Growing Up Rich in a Poor Family

Growing Up Rich in a Poor Family

Childhood Memories from the Great Depression

Doris Hermundstad Liffrig

Melissa Gordon, Illustrator

iUniverse, Inc.
Bloomington

Growing Up Rich in a Poor Family
Childhood Memories from the Great Depression

iUniverse books may be ordered through booksellers or by contacting:

iUniverse
1663 Liberty Drive
Bloomington, IN 47403
www.iuniverse.com
1-800-Authors (1-800-288-4677)

Illustrations by Melissa Gordon

ISBN: 978-1-4620-3209-9 (sc)
ISBN: 978-1-4620-3210-5 (e)

Printed in the United States of America

iUniverse rev. date: 11/15/2011

I thank fate
for having made me born poor.
Poverty taught me
the true value
of the gifts useful to life.

—Anonymous

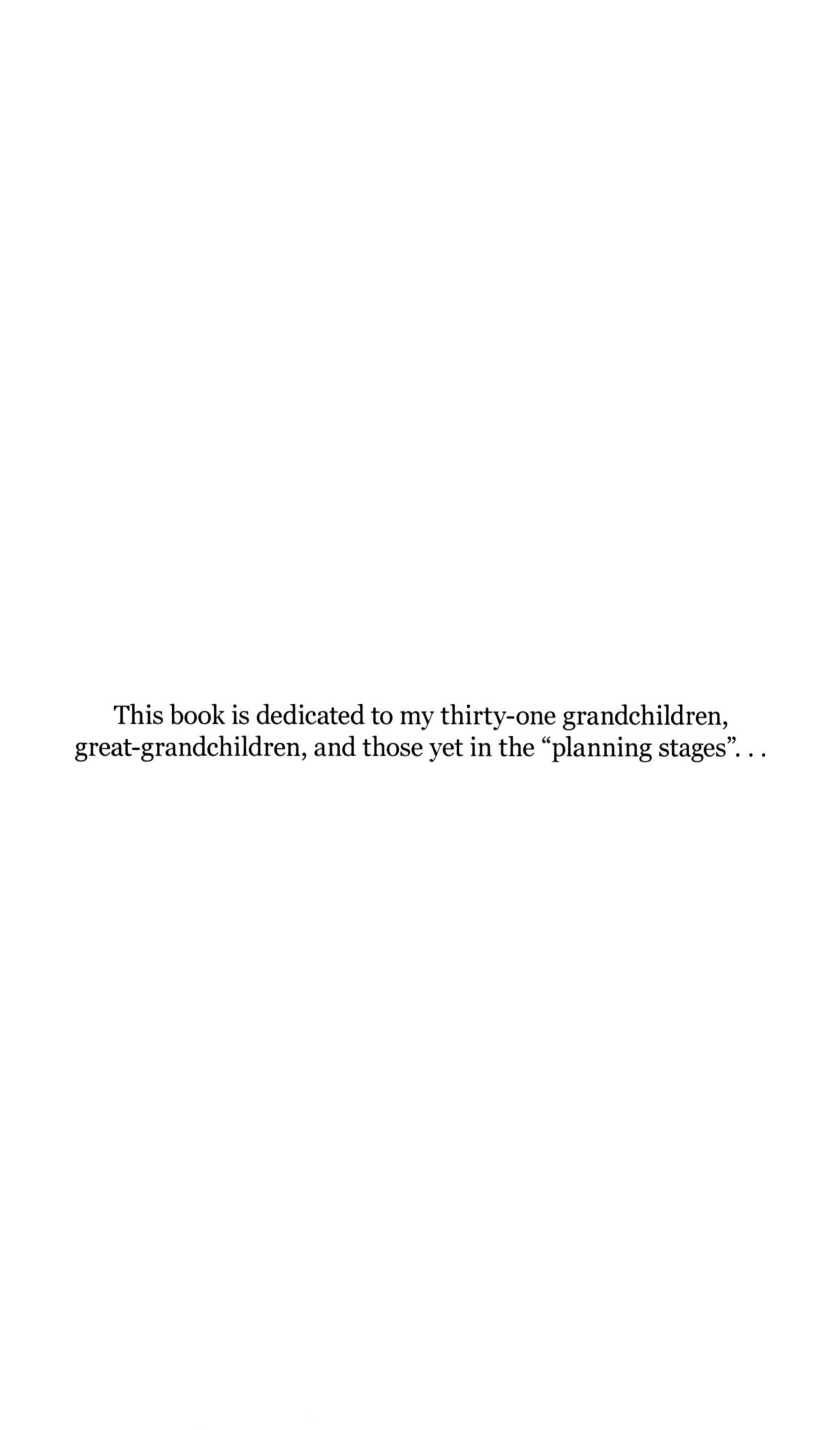

This book is dedicated to my thirty-one grandchildren, great-grandchildren, and those yet in the "planning stages". . .

Contents

Acknowledgments

Special thanks to Duane, a patient, interested husband, who has willingly and cheerfully overlooked late meals, put aside meetings and appointments, and offered suggestions and information upon request for the sake of this book.

Also, to my daughter, Julie Fedorchak, a professional writer, who has taken time out of her busy life to edit, correct, and replace words and phrases in the original text.

Your encouragement and confidence have made the difference!

For Julia—my inspiration,
Mom—my motivation,
and Bob, my foundation.
~Melissa

Preface

The stories I am sharing in *Growing Up Rich in a Poor Family* are memories I have from growing up during the Great Depression of the 1930s. I hope these stories will help my children, grandchildren and great-grandchildren better understand and appreciate this time period. Having only one toy is unheard of in today's world, but it forced children years ago to be creative and frugal. One box of eight crayons had to last a year. How many times I recall coloring a pretty paper napkin, being ever so careful not to tear it, or tracing a picture from a book or magazine in the window and then coloring it.

We lived on a farm on the prairies of western North Dakota, where years went by without rain, the dust blew day and night, Russian thistles served as Christmas trees, and bony cows were sold for lack of feed. I can close my eyes today and see my father sitting on the step of the windmill by the pump on summer evenings, with little hope that the clouds rolling by would produce rain.

My family consisted of my parents, Olga and John; my two brothers, Jerold and Orin; and me. Looking back, I realize how difficult our lives were. But the childhood experiences I relate in this book set the course for my life, and I wouldn't change my humble beginnings for anything.

I had a wonderful time in my own private world of make-believe. I treasured Betsy, my naked doll and only toy. She and I shared many hours of fun and togetherness. As you read these stories, I hope you, too, will gain a better understanding of the day-to-day struggle that was necessary to survive the Great Depression and the community life that knit the neighbors together as family.

A Little Girl Named Doris and Her Brothers, Jerold and Orin

Once upon a time, a long time ago now, there was a little girl named Doris. Her mama sometimes called her "Toots," and her oldest brother almost always called her "Suzie." Her father pronounced her name "Dord-eez," with a heavy Norwegian accent. Her daddy, she was told, had come from Norway, where he had lived in a big house with an upstairs. *How lucky*, Doris thought when she looked at the pictures.

Doris lived on a farm with her mama, Olga; her daddy, John; and two brothers, Jerold and Orin. Their tar-papered* house was very small, just one big room. Doris hated the tar paper. *Nobody else I know has tar paper on their house. Why do we?* Doris moaned to herself, embarrassment tormenting her whenever anyone drove into the yard.

Close to the house were a windmill, a fence, and a water tank for the cattle and horses. Scattered throughout the yard were two granaries, a barn ready to fall down, a car shed, a pigpen, a chicken coop, and a shed for the Model T.

---

* Heavy, oiled paper nailed with slats onto the outside of a house

Doris did not have a bedroom in which to keep her things separate from her brothers'. She dreamed and dreamed of a bigger house, a house big enough for her to have her own space.

If I had my own bedroom with my own dresser drawers, I would be the happiest girl in the whole wide world, she thought. She would even help her mama with the dishes every day without complaining. Doris frequently slept at the foot of her parents' bed. She often went to sleep at night thinking about a house like the one in Norway in which her daddy had grown up.

Maybe someday we'll have a house with an upstairs, she thought as she drifted off to sleep. *A house with my own bedroom, my own bureau with drawers, my own window. Just mine and nobody else's. Just mine.*

Eventually a cot was put in the corner of the main house for her.

"Mama! Do I get my very own bed?" Doris exclaimed. She was thrilled when Olga said yes. Finally, she had a place to lay her doll, a place where she could put precious things under her pillow and on the floor under the cot.

Jerold and Orin were older than Doris. Jerold was seven, Orin was six, and Doris was five. Her brothers shared a closet-sized room that was large enough for only a bed and a chest of drawers tucked behind the door. There wasn't enough room to open the outside door, so it wasn't used.

Doris had one drawer in the chest. It was better than nothing, but sharing with her brothers was discouraging. They sometimes snooped in her drawer, and her mama never did one thing about it!

Jerold and Orin loved the privacy of their tiny room. There wasn't much space to move around, but the room had one key feature: a door. This closed out the activity and noise from the rest of the house and secluded Orin and Jerold from their meddling little sister.

Chores for Everyone

Doris had chores to do every day. On Monday, she helped her mama with the laundry. This was a big job, because their farmhouse didn't have running water. John carried the hot water from the boiler* on the stove to the Maytag washer, while Olga cut pieces of soap into the tub from a bar of P&G.† John started the machine by stepping on the motor pedal. He had to be careful not to choke the motor with too much gas. If this happened, the machine would not start, and Olga would have to wait for half an hour or more for the motor to cool.

Doris did most of the rinsing in a tub of cold water and learned to put the clean, rinsed clothes through the wringer, which she liked to do, especially on hot days.

The last load was always the work clothes; sometimes a rug and dirty rags were thrown in. By then, the water in the washing machine was almost black. In spite of this, the leftover water was used to scrub the floor.

Doris helped hang the clean clothes on the line and took them in when they were dry. *Carrying clothes to and from the line is hard work*, she thought. It took several trips to haul the clean, fresh-smelling clothes into the house, where Doris piled them in a heap on the bed. She helped Mama fold and put them away.

Olga showed her how to sprinkle whatever needed ironing. "Don't sprinkle too much," she warned, "or it will be hard to

---

* Large, covered copper container used for heating water

† A large bar of laundry soap

iron them dry. Roll them tight, and wrap them in a sheet. They will be ready to iron in an hour."

Ironing meant heating heavy, flat irons* on the stove. On the days Olga ironed, the house became very hot. During the summer, ironing often took two afternoons. Sometimes, Olga let Doris iron easy pieces like handkerchiefs, pillowcases, dish towels, and aprons. Doris felt important when she ironed, especially when she folded and pressed a pillowcase just right.

"Oh, that's nice, Doris. You did a good job. No wrinkles, and you didn't scorch† anything." This was often a problem with the heavy flat irons.

Doris also helped Olga wash and dry the dishes, pick weeds from the garden, and sweep the floor, and she made her bed every morning. When Olga baked bread or cookies, Doris helped stir and knead the bread—and lick the spoon.

Jerold and Orin worked outside with John. They milked cows, cleaned the barn, separated the milk, and fed the pigs, calves, and chickens. Hauling wood and coal for the stoves was a daily chore, as was carrying out the ashes from the stoves. During the summer, the two boys helped with haying, shocking‡ the grain, and herding§ the cows.

One of the chores that all three kids detested was picking mustard in the fields.

"We better have the kids help pick mustard this morning before it gets too hot," John told his wife one summer morning.

---

* Heavy, metal, diamond-shaped irons with a snap-on wooden handle

† Holding the flat iron too long, therefore burning the garment or piece

‡ Stacking five or six bundles of grain into an upright pyramid

§ Watching cattle in a distant field

Olga hated the job as much as her three little kids, but she knew it had to be done. The crop could not grow with so many weeds choking it. Even though it was already blistering hot, she told Jerold, Orin, and Doris what their daddy had said. "Hurry, now, and eat your breakfast," Olga told them. "We have to get out there before it gets much hotter."

Jerold and Orin loved to take their time eating their Wheaties, the breakfast of champions, and looking at the pictures on the box. Today was different.

"Get your hats, and we'll go to the field as soon as you finish your cereal. Hurry—Daddy is waiting."

It was an endless, monotonous, tiring job. They picked for hours, yet the field still looked full of the pesky yellow weeds. Doris thought the bright flowers were pretty and wondered why she had to pick them.

By mid-afternoon, John said they could quit. Even though the three kids were hungry and tired, they ran to the house to get out of the sun.

"Hey, Orin, let's ask Mama if we can go swimming," Jerold yelled.

"Yeah, let's!" Orin called back as they raced to the house.

Olga reluctantly agreed to their plan but worried, as always, about the water in the slough, which was deep enough for them to drown.

"Jerold, you watch and make sure Doris and Orin stay on this side of the fence."

"Okay, Mama."

The three kids loved jumping into the cool water and covering themselves with mud, never giving a thought to the idea that it was the same water the cows stood in on the other side of the fence.

During the summer, the small house was stiflingly hot. Flies swarmed in and out as soon as the door was opened. Lady, the dog, could not decide whether she was better off inside or outside. Jerold answered her frequent scratching at the door many times during the evening

Winters were cold in the house. Rags stuffed in the windows helped to keep out the wind. John and the boys hauled manure from the barn to spread around the house's foundation for insulation before winter set in. A potbelly* stove sat in the middle of the room, and a kitchen range was at the other end of the house.

Olga often spent evenings sitting on an armless rocking chair by the potbelly stove, doing handwork. The boys played with trucks under the bed or with marbles on top of the bed. Doris drew and colored pictures or played house with her doll on her cot. Popcorn, popped in a kettle on top of the kitchen range, was a special treat on cold winter evenings. Doris loved playing horsey on her daddy's knee or sharing an apple while she sat on his lap, listening to the radio together.

When unexpected company came, the men folk sat on the few available chairs, and the ladies sat on the bed to visit. "You kids go outside and play," the kids were instructed, regardless of season.

Grandma and Grandpa Kvam, aunts and uncles, and many cousins lived nearby. Going the sixteen miles to Grandma's house or the twenty to visit aunts and uncles took almost an hour, but the young family still enjoyed frequent visits.

Occasionally, Olga and Doris took time to visit the neighbors. One day, they decided to visit the Maurers. As they were driving on the dirt road toward the Maurers' place, Doris asked, "Mama, how many kids do the Maurers have?"

---

* A small, round, iron heater that uses wood or coal for fuel

"I think they have ten," Olga replied. "Why are you asking?"

"I was wondering how many brothers and sisters Ada and Evelyn have." Doris liked playing with Ada and Evelyn, as they were about the same age.

As they drove into the yard, they saw Mrs. Maurer outside, getting a pail of water from the well. She set the pail down by the door and walked to the car.

"Doris and I decided at the last minute to come over for a cup of coffee," Olga told her as she got out of the car.

Mrs. Maurer seemed pleased. "Oh, please come in. I haven't sat down since I got up early this morning."

Their house is bigger than ours, Doris thought as she walked in, *but why are the walls not finished and the floor dirt?* Doris hadn't been in the Maurers' house very often. It surprised her again to see the dirt floor.

Mrs. Maurer put the coffeepot on and told Ada and Evelyn to stop folding the clothes. "Doris is here, so you can finish your job later. You girls go play."

Mrs. Maurer and Olga sat down to visit. Mrs. Maurer thanked Olga for the huge plate of cookies she'd brought. Olga told Mrs. Maurer they would only stay a short time. "I know you have work to do before supper," Olga said.

When they headed home, Doris asked, "Mama, how come the Maurers don't have a floor in their house?"

Olga didn't answer right away. She looked at Doris and finally said, "Well, they have a large family, and they just don't have money for a floor."

Doris was very quiet as Olga drove back to their farm. She looked out of the window and muttered to herself, "Well, at least we have a floor."

When Olga turned into their yard, Doris looked at the

shanty* on their house. It, too, had a dirt floor. Most houses that Doris had seen did not have a shanty, and no one but the Maurers had a dirt floor. Doris wondered if they were poor like the Maurers but decided not to ask.

Despite the hardships and lack of conveniences, the families in the neighborhood were supportive of and concerned for one another. What they didn't have was never missed. What they had was cherished and treasured. Little kids learned early in life to save and be creative. Doris, Orin, and Jerold were no exception.

---

* An unfinished shed attached to a house or building, frequently without a floor

A Penny from Heaven

One day, when Olga and Doris were in town, they had time to look around in Lohman's Store. Olga was looking at and pricing a pair of stockings for Doris. Doris needed new shoes, too, but Olga knew there was no money to buy them right now. Doris walked right over to the counter to look at the dolls and doll dishes. She knew exactly where they were, as she had looked at them many times before. Doris had only one doll, and it was her favorite playmate. She and Betsy spent much of their time in the brooder house* or the Little Red House.† Doris used tin cans, jar lids, flat stones, and sticks for dishes and silverware, and she longed for a set of real dishes.

She took one of the plates out of the box to look at the flowers. Mrs. Lohman noticed and came hustling over. "Do not touch these dishes!" she said sternly, grabbing the plate out of Doris's hand. Doris ran to her mother and stood behind her.

---

* A small round structure used for keeping newly hatched chicks warm

† A small, closed building used for setting hens, christened "the Little Red House" by the kids

Doris was among the many children during the Depression who saved pennies. She kept them in a small jar and counted them almost every day. After a long time, she had saved ninety-nine pennies. She was very excited and wondered how and when she could get just one more. She ran to the kitchen to tell her mama the good news. "Mama! I only need one more penny, and then I will have a dollar—a whole dollar for the dishes, Mama!"

"Oh, my, Doris. That's wonderful!" Olga said as she was washing dishes.

"Maybe when Torvald comes, he will give me a penny. Do you think he will, Mama?" Doris asked eagerly. Mama smiled and nodded.

Torvald was a bachelor who lived four miles directly east of them. He didn't drive, so he walked everywhere. Torvald had come from Norway, like many of the other settlers in the area. Because he didn't have a wife or family, he'd never learned to speak English. He did not have a telephone, radio, or any books, magazines, or papers, because he could not read English.

He frequently walked the four miles to visit John and Olga, because both of them could understand and speak Norwegian. Many of his other close neighbors spoke only German. Torvald also seemed to like the three little farm kids, and he usually brought a treat for them. He smiled when they shook his hand and thanked him. Otherwise, he just sat in the chair and watched Olga and the kids.

Then one day it happened.

A knock on the door one afternoon surprised both Doris and Olga. Doris looked out the window by the door and saw Torvald. "Mama! It's Torvald. Torvald is at the door." Doris immediately had visions of getting the penny she needed for the doll dishes.

"Ask Torvald to come in and sit down," she told Doris. "Tell him Daddy should be home soon."

Torvald was able to understand a few words of English, especially if it related to John. Torvald sat down and watched Olga working in the kitchen rolling out doughnuts. Torvald's diet consisted mostly of salt pork and bread. When Olga finished the frying, she poured a cup of coffee and offered him three doughnuts. "*Vasha go,*"* Olga said, smiling.

Torvald ate as many as Olga offered. The three doughnuts on the plate quickly disappeared. Torvald kept repeating, "*Mange takk. Tusen takk.*"† Doris understood a few Norwegian words, especially *thanks.*

When Doris finished coloring a picture in her coloring book, she showed it to Torvald. "See," she said, "it's a picture of Popeye, Wimpy, and Olive Oyl.‡ You can have it." She handed it to Torvald. He smiled and said something in Norwegian to Olga that Doris didn't understand. Then he stood up and reached into his pocket.

Oh, goody, Doris thought. *I'm going to get a penny.* Instead, Torvald handed Doris a piece of Horehound candy. Doris's mouth fell open. She hated Horehound candy. To her, it tasted like medicine. Nevertheless, she shook Torvald's hand, tried to smile, and said, "*Mange takk.*"

Then her face turned from glad to sad. She had convinced herself that she would get what she was hoping for. "Now I'll never get my penny," she told Mama, heartbroken, as she handed Olga the bitter candy.

"It's okay, Doris," Olga said, trying to console her. "I know you

---

* "Help yourself."

† "Many thanks. Thousand thanks."

‡ Characters in a comic book

were expecting a penny, but don't be discouraged. Something will turn up. We must learn to be patient."

Torvald smiled as he took his fourth doughnut. "*Tusen takk,*" he said. He reached into his pocket for two more pieces of Horehound candy. "*Vasha go til Jerold and Orin.*"

Doris knew what he meant. She took the candy, thanked him, and then put the candy on a shelf in the little bedroom. *I wonder when Torvald will come back,* she wondered. Doris couldn't think of anyone else who might give her a penny. *Neither Grandma nor Uncle Genald ever gave me money. And Daddy only gives me a penny for church on Sunday*, she thought. She decided to forget about it and went back to coloring another picture.

Torvald went outside when he heard John drive into the yard. "*Mange tusen takk,*" he told Olga as he went out the door.

Every day after that, Doris watched for Torvald on the road. A week went by. Then another. Then, one day, as she was hanging clothes on the clothesline, she saw someone walking toward their farm. Doris watched a little longer before she ran into the house. "Mama! Mama, Torvald is coming!"

Olga wasn't nearly as excited as Doris and was relieved that John was home to talk with him. Doris ran to the barn to tell her daddy that Torvald was almost at their mailbox.

The two farmers began talking farm business in Norwegian. John invited Torvald in for coffee. Doris set the table with cups and a plate with fresh bread, butter, and sugar.

"Doris, get the sugar lumps* from the cupboard," John said. Doris was eager to hang around Torvald. All she could think about was getting a penny.

"*Mange takk,*" Torvald said and reached into his pocket.

---

* Square cubes of sugar to be dipped in hot coffee.

Doris held her breath, hoping he was not going to give her more Horehound candy. He told Doris what a nice little girl she was and then put a penny into her hand. Doris wanted to jump up and down and scream, but she merely shook Torvald's hand, said "*Tusen takk*," and ran to the corner to retrieve her penny jar from under the cot. She was quite sure this penny meant she had a dollar. She dumped them all out and started counting. Torvald watched as she counted all the way to one hundred. Doris couldn't contain her excitement. She hurried to the kitchen.

"Mama! Mama! I have a dollar!"

Torvald had not expected such a joyful response and did not understand what Doris said to Olga. He just sat very erect, smiling, leaning with both hands on his walking stick. John and Torvald finished their coffee and went outside.

Olga was not surprised. "A dollar, Doris? Good for you. You have been so good about saving all your pennies. Daddy will be proud of you."

Doris spread her pennies on the cot and counted them again, just to make sure she had counted right. Doris had wanted the doll dishes at Lohman's Store for a very, very long time. The day after Torvald's visit, Olga told Doris they had to go to town for a few groceries.

"Mama, can we go into Lohman's and buy the doll dishes?"

"Are you sure you have enough money?" Olga questioned.

"Yes, Mama. The box was marked one dollar, and now I have a dollar. I've counted three times to make sure."

"Okay. We'll go there after we get groceries."

When they went into Lohman's Store, Mrs. Lohman followed them to the counter where the box of dishes was displayed. She wouldn't let Doris pick them up and seemed very surprised when Olga told her Doris wanted to buy them.

"Doris has been saving her pennies for many months. She finally has enough to buy these dishes. She's been looking at them since Christmas," Olga told Mrs. Lohman proudly.

Mrs. Lohman was generally very crabby, but when Doris gave her one hundred pennies, she smiled and handed her the box of dishes securely tied with string. Doris took the box, said "Thank you," and carefully carried it to the car. She could hardly wait to get home.

Doris and her doll had tea parties every day. When Torvald came to their house a couple of weeks later, Doris invited him to her tea party. He didn't really understand, but he nodded his head and smiled. Having pretend coffee with dolls and doll dishes was completely foreign to this Norwegian bachelor. But he smiled and played along. Olga had given Doris a few doughnut holes to serve with her pretend coffee, and Torvald would do just about anything for the chance to have some of Olga's delicious doughnuts.

"Mama! A Tramp Is Coming Over the Hill!"

Tramps during the Great Depression were men who left their families out of desperation and became beggars and hobos. They were most often hungry and usually harmless. They carried their only belongings in a small sack tied to a stick and placed over their shoulder. Jerold was in the barn, putting hay in the stalls for the cows, when he noticed a tramp heading toward their farm.

"Mama!" Jerold hollered as he ran into the house. "Mama! A tramp is coming over the hill behind the barn!"

"Where? Are you sure? Where is he? Is he close?" Olga said nervously, a look of panic plainly visible on her face. Olga, alone in the house, alone on the farm with her three little kids, was scared to death of tramps. John was gone, and Orin was outside by the water tank, getting a drink. "Get in the house, Orin. Quick! A tramp is coming," Olga yelled. "Hurry! Hurry! Where is Doris? Jerold, go find her. Run!"

Jerold ran around outside, hollering almost loudly enough for the tramp to hear. "Doris! Doris! Where are you? A tramp is coming. Mama wants you in the house right now."

Doris was playing with her dolls in the old chicken coop, which she had renamed the Little Red House. She came out when she heard Jerold yelling and ran to the house as fast as she could. She was afraid of tramps, too, just like her mama.

"Orin and Doris, get in the closet. You, too, Jerold. Hurry! Don't come out until I tell you. And be quiet—don't say a word." Olga was shaking.

Jerold, Orin, and Doris had done this before, and, because Olga was so frightened, they were, too. Especially Doris. They stood motionless in the dark closet, not daring to move or make a peep.

Olga grabbed two butcher knives and quickly shut the door. She slid the knives into the doorframe against the door and hoped the knives would hold the door shut so the tramp couldn't break it open. She went to the window, pulled the shade, hid behind the curtain, and waited.

She heard footsteps, then the knock. "Be quiet, kids. He's here!" she whispered.

The knock came again and again. She heard the doorknob being turned and jiggled back and forth. A pause. Then kicks on the door, followed by more knocks and another kick. Finally, silence. Just as Olga was about to come out from the behind the curtain, another knock sounded, louder than the others. "Shhh! Be still, kids. He's still here," she whispered a little louder.

Barely breathing, Olga waited until she was sure the coast was clear. She slowly ventured from behind the curtain, tiptoed to the window, and carefully pulled the curtain back a few inches. She watched the man, a knapsack on his back, walk to the road. He turned toward Caseys' house, and Olga breathed a huge sigh of relief.

She tiptoed and watched the tramp walk past Holmens' mailbox and on to the west. "It's okay now, kids. You can come out. The tramp is gone. He's heading toward Caseys," she said finally.

Fright was still evident in her eyes. The three kids came out of the closet, but Olga would not let them go outside for fear the tramp might return. She realized that was highly unlikely, but she wasn't about to take any chances.

It was hot in the house, and the boys wanted to finish the chores John had assigned before he came back from the field.

Doris had “company” waiting for her in the Little Red House for a tea party.

“Can’t we go outside now, Mama?” Jerold persisted. “The tramp is gone. If Caseys aren’t home, he’ll head for Jordets’ house.”

Finally, Olga decided that half an hour was long enough. “Okay. Go finish the chores,” she said.

When John came home that evening, Doris was the first to run out to the truck and tell him what had happened. “Daddy! A tramp came, and we had to hide in the closet for a long time.”

John understood and realized how frightened Olga was of these men. “What happened?” he asked. “Did Mama give him some food?”

“No,” Doris explained. “We had to hide in the closet for a long time.”

“It’s okay now, Doris,” John said. “I’m home, and I’m not afraid of tramps.”

When John walked into the house, Olga told him that another tramp had come to their place and that she and the kids had hidden in the house. “I know, Olga. Doris already told me.”

John’s attitude to tramps was far different from his wife’s. When John was home, the tramp always received a plate of food. Luckily, John was home for the next tramp’s visit. This time, the tramp arrived from the west. John shook his hand and asked if he needed food.

“Sure do,” he answered. “Haven’t eaten for two days.”

John told Jerold to go tell Mama to get some food ready for him. Jerold quickly obeyed and hurried back outside. He didn’t want to miss any part of the tramp’s story.

“How long you been on the road?” John asked.

“Oh, I don’t keep much track of time,” the tramp replied.

"Reckon it's been a few months. I been gone since before Christmas."

"Where you from?"

"Me and my family lived in Oklahoma. But things got tough there. Couldn't find work. Everybody hungry. No jobs. Nothin' to look forward to, so I left. Told my wife I'd try to send her some money to help take care of the kids, but haven't had much luck so far findin' work." Every tramp had a similar story. Desperate, hopeless, and hungry.

"What's happened to your family? Your wife and kids?"

"I dunno. Haven't heard from 'em." He looked at the ground.

Clearly the man felt bad, but John wondered how hard he had tried to find work. Living the life of a bum and riding the rails seemed like an easy way out, a lot easier than trying to feed and clothe your family.

Olga found whatever leftovers she felt she could spare and handed the plate to John. The tramp sat on the running board of the car and ate hungrily. The man was obviously starving. Orin, Jerold, and Doris felt safe standing close by their dad and loved to listen to the tramp talk about his life.

"What do you plan on doing?" John prodded. He hoped the man hadn't given up on life and his family.

"All I can do is ride the rails and hope somethin' turns up," the tramp said skeptically. He finished his food quickly and handed the plate to John. "Thank ye. I sure do appreciate you helpin' me."

John knew he could have eaten another plateful of food but also knew they couldn't spare any more. His own kids were hungry.

The tramp stood up and shook John's hand. He patted the

three kids on their heads and said, "Be good now. Your daddy's a good man."

John wished him luck.

After he left, Olga put his plate, cup, and fork in boiling water for half an hour. She didn't trust these tramps or care about their reasons for needing food. She felt there was no excuse for any man leaving his wife and kids, and she didn't much care how hungry the tramps were. In her mind, they probably weren't nearly as hungry as the families they'd abandoned.

"I Hear the Lump Now, Mama!"

Churning butter was one of the jobs Olga decided six-year-old Doris was old enough to handle.

Doris was eating breakfast: a bowl of Wheaties with a sprinkle of sugar and milk brimming to the top. She could also have a piece of toast if she toasted the bread on the hot stove. "Can I have some jelly?" she asked.

"Not today, Doris," Olga said. "But you can have butter and sugar." Doris decided to skip the toast.

"Doris, don't forget, we churn butter today," Olga reminded her.

Doris, studying the pictures of kids eating Wheaties on back of the box, barely heard what her mama said. She almost choked on a large spoonful of cereal. Looking up, she said, "But, Mama, you told me I could play with Catherine this afternoon!"

"I know. You can go later, after we finish churning,"* Olga said calmly.

Doris was disappointed. She had told Catherine the day before that she could play in the afternoon. By the time she got

* Turing the handle of a large wooden barrel that rested on a stand until the cream turned into butter

the cream churned, she knew half of the afternoon would be gone.

Catherine Casey was Doris's best friend. Not only were they the same age, but they lived walking distance from each other and played together often. And they both had red hair. Catherine's mother kept her only daughter's hair long in naturally curly ringlets. Olga kept Doris's hair short because it was perfectly straight. Doris also had many more freckles than her friend. Doris was always envious of her friend's pretty hair, and she hated her freckles because Catherine had very few.

Catherine had three brothers, all older than Doris's two brothers, Jerold and Orin. Occasionally, if John and Olga wanted to go somewhere after supper, one of the Casey boys came to watch the kids. Doris secretly hoped Dick would come. He was the most fun. The Casey family did not have a telephone or radio, so Catherine's brothers liked coming when John or Olga asked for help. Once Jerold, Orin, and Doris were in bed, the caretaker could listen to the radio for the rest of the evening.

Catherine's family was also poor and lived in a small house with only one bedroom. Like Doris, Catherine slept on a cot in a corner by the dining room table. Catherine didn't like playing house with dolls, so the two friends played school or hopscotch or made up games to play outside or in the barn.

At one o'clock, Doris reminded Olga to get her job started so she could play. "Can I start churning before we do the dishes, Mama?" Doris knew the suggestion was probably not an option, but she thought Mama might give in this one time.

"No, Doris. We do dishes as soon as we finish eating."

By the sound of her voice, Doris knew the discussion was over. Olga's days were filled with a variety of ongoing jobs—washing clothes; ironing; baking bread, cookies, cakes, or doughnuts; gardening; mending; sewing; scrubbing the floor;

washing windows; and filling the lamps with kerosene.* Cooking supper with a dishpan full of dirty dishes merely added to her frustration.

When the dishes were finished, Olga pulled the churn from behind the door and set it close to the window. The churn was a large wooden barrel on a frame, with a crank-type handle. A cork plugged the hole at the bottom of the barrel, and fasteners were attached to the top of the churn to clamp the cover on securely.

"Doris, get the cream from the cellar," Mama said. "But be very careful not to drop the pail. We can't afford to spill the cream."

Doris opened the cellar door and went down the steep, narrow steps. She never liked going into the dark, damp cellar. She had seen spiders, mice and even a lizard or two crawling on the dirt floor and decided it was a creepy place. She found the covered cream pail on the floor and started back up the steps. Olga stood by the open door and quickly grabbed the pail.

At times, depending on the temperature and richness of the cream, it took an hour or longer for the cream to turn into butter. Other times, it took only half an hour. Doris was hoping today was one of those lucky times.

Olga liked to use sweet cream for better-tasting butter, even if it did take longer to churn. She poured the cream into the churn and made sure the cover was on tightly and the cork was pushed firmly into the opening at the bottom of the churn. "Okay, Doris. It's ready. You can start churning now," she called to Doris, who had started coloring a picture in her coloring book.

---

* Kerosene, a mixture of carbons distilled from petroleum used in lamps

Doris began turning the crank. After a turn, she noticed some cream oozing out of the cover, but she ignored it. She didn't want churning to take up her valuable playtime. She made a couple more turns and then hollered, "Mama! Come quick. There's cream on the floor."

Olga was there in an instant. "Stop!" she yelled. Luckily, the cover, which was not fastened tightly, hadn't worked itself completely loose. "Doris! How many times have I told you to check the cover before you begin turning the crank?"

Doris knew better, but she just hadn't wanted to take the time to do it.

"You were just lucky this time, and you better not let it happen again, or you'll spend the afternoon mopping up cream rather than playing with Catherine!"

Doris remembered a time when it had happened and stopped complaining. She certainly didn't want to have to help her mama mop up slippery cream. She decided she'd better be more careful, even if Catherine was waiting.

Doris had learned to start churning slowly. The cream rolled around better, she'd been told. Doris kept the cream moving, even if her arms got tired. After half an hour, she thought she could *feel* the cream getting thick. *If that was happening, it wouldn't take long to get butter,* she thought. She began turning the barrel faster and faster. "Mama, I think I can hear the lump!" Doris called as she kept the churn moving. She could hear and feel a chunk sloshing around in the churn. "Mama! It's done. I hear a lump in the buttermilk!"

Olga pushed the kettle of chokecherries to the back of the stove and checked the churning's progress. "Yes, I think you're right. Let me do a couple of turns just to make sure." Doris was right. Smiling, Olga said, "You're getting to be a pretty good butter churner, Doris."

Doris didn't much care if she was a good churner or not. All she wanted was to be done with the job so she could run to Catherine's house.

Olga found a jar to drain the buttermilk. She pulled the cork while Doris tilted the barrel to get every drop out of the churn.

"Am I done, Mama? Can I go now? I hope Catherine is still waiting."

"As soon as you clean the churn," Olga replied. She brought a crock and paddle to remove the chunk of butter. Doris held onto the churn as she was told.

"Clean the churn? Now? Can't I do it later?"

"Doris, you know the churn has to be cleaned as soon as we drain the buttermilk."

Doris quickly got warm water from the reservoir* on the stove, some soap, and a clean rag to scrub the inside of the churn. When she was sure it was clean, she threw the water outside on the other side of the milk house and got clean water from the water tank. She rinsed the rags, hung them up on the clothesline, and dumped the rinse water on the garden. "I'm done, Mama. *Now* can I go?" Doris asked.

"Go ahead," Olga replied. "But be home by 4:30."

Doris flew out the door and started running down the road. Catherine was watching for her friend. She finally saw her and ran to meet her.

"I had to churn butter before I could play," Doris explained. "Then Mama made me clean the churn."

"I know."

---

* A large container on the side of the kitchen range for hot water storage

Catherine understood. She always had chores to do, too. The two friends decided to play in the barn and climbed into the hayloft to decide what they should play. Sometimes they just sat in the soft hay and talked while watching the horses. Catherine's big brother Jack loved horses and had taught Catherine to ride. Coming from Norway, Doris's daddy was not used to horses. Consequently, they had only two work horses, which no one could ride.

"Is it fun to ride?" Doris asked.

"Oh, lots of fun," Catherine answered. "Especially when you can gallop. Do you want to try?"

"Oh, no! Mama told me to never get on a horse."

The girls decided to go back to the house to play school. All too soon, Catherine's mother told them it was almost four thirty and time for Doris to go home.

That night and for the next few days, the family enjoyed fresh garden vegetables smothered in butter, homemade cakes and frostings, popcorn, and fresh warm bread covered with butter and sugar. Fresh buttermilk was one of John's favorite treats.

A Tale about Herding Cows

The morning was already hot. Olga told Jerold and Orin to hurry and eat their breakfast so they could start their work before the temperature climbed higher. Olga had set a pitcher of milk, a bowl of sugar, a box of Wheaties, and some bread on the table. The boys looked at pictures of Jack Armstrong* on the cereal box as they ate. Orin refilled his bowl, trying to stall as long as he could.

"Get your hats now, boys, and get going!" Olga said sternly. She was familiar with their stalling tactics, even though she empathized with their reasons. Without a doubt, herding cattle was a tedious job, taking the boys more than a mile from their house to a pasture where grass was more plentiful. Entertaining themselves on the job for several hours a day was an ongoing challenge for these seven- and eight-year-old boys.

"It's time to go," Olga announced again. "Hurry up, now! The sun is already blistering. And don't forget your water jug."

"Why doesn't Doris have to go?" Orin asked. "Just because she's a girl doesn't mean she should get out of everything," he grumbled as he looked for his straw hat.

---

* The host of a popular radio show for young listeners

Olga had packed a lunch bucket with *spekkjott,*[*] buttered bread, two doughnuts for each of them, and a surprise—an all-day sucker.[†] "Be careful," Olga told the boys. "And watch the cows so they don't get into the neighbor's wheat field. Be sure to keep your hats on." She watched them let the cows out of the gate.

"I'll close the gate, Jerold. You and Orin go. When the sun gets over the Caseys' house, you can start for home." Orin clapped and yelled from behind.

As she watched the boys cross the road, Doris thought of the rhyme Mama had read to her many times. She jumped on her swing and watched the cows get smaller and smaller as she sailed higher and higher. She repeated the rhyme over and over: "Little Boy Blue, come blow your horn. The sheep's in the meadow; the cow's in the corn."

Olga soon interrupted her cool journey into the sky. "Doris, you have to come and wash the separator[‡] now."

"Right now, Mama? Can I wait a while?"

"Now!" Mama insisted.

Doris hated washing the separator. It had so many parts, including dozens and dozens of steel disks, and Mama was very fussy about each one being washed and dried. But, like Orin, Doris had to do things she didn't like. *I wish Orin was here to see what I have to do. I bet he wouldn't think I was such a baby,* she thought as she set the dishpan of hot water outside

---

[*] Beef soaked in brine and then hung to dry for two to three months

[†] A large sucker sold in stores for a penny

[‡] Machine turned by a crank that spins milk through steel disks that separate the cream from the milk

the wash house.[*] The separator had to be washed twice a day, and it was usually Doris's job.

In the late afternoon, Doris spotted the boys across the road, coming home. She ran to the house to tell Olga. "Mama, the boys are coming home with the cows." Her mother looked at the clock. It was already close to six.

The next day, John said the boys should take the cows to another area closer to their farm. "I'll have Doris bring you some cookies and nectar[†] around ten thirty," Olga told the boys as they put their straw hats on. "Then one of you can come home for a while."

A car sped by just as Jerold and Orin crossed the road with the cows, leaving a long trail of dust. The boys rubbed their eyes and noses as they headed east. They liked this site much more, not only because it was closer to the house but because there was always the possibility that their friend and neighbor DuWayne would be herding cattle nearby.

"Well, at least we might have someone to talk to for a while today," Jerold told Orin. They took a storybook and some playing cards along just in case.

They were there less than an hour when Orin spotted DuWayne and his sister Marlys heading their way. The friends greeted one another enthusiastically. Even though they lived only a mile apart, neither farm family could afford much playtime for their kids. The outlook for prairie farms was bleak, and everyone—young and old—had to help keep their family farm alive.

An hour or more passed before the herders found relief from the sun's persistent rays. Jerold was the first to discover

---

[*] A small building close to the house where separating and clothes washing were done

[†] A concentrated flavored syrup mixed with water

the culvert beneath the gravel highway that separated the two farms. “Hey, come in here!” he yelled. “It’s cool. It’s like a tunnel.”

The herders made their way slowly and cautiously, exploring the new hideaway, which was full of Russian thistles.* DuWayne entered timidly from the other end. Suddenly he shrieked and ran back out toward daylight.

“Look out! There’s a skunk in there.”

The kids scrambled for the other end of the culvert while the original occupant took off in the opposite direction, leaving his scent behind.

“Wow, that was a close call,” Jerold said. “Did you guys get hit?”

Fortunately, the skunk had missed them all with its horrific-smelling spray.

---

* A round, prickly plant that blew over the prairies during the Depression

Later, when the blistering sun began to take its toll again, Orin, Jerold, DuWayne, and Marlys wondered if they dared go back into the cool hideaway. Then Orin noticed his sister coming across the field.

"Mama sent some fresh cookies and cold water," Doris said when she reached the cow herders. "And you can go home now, Orin. She said I should stay until noon."

But to Orin, the excitement of exploring the culvert seemed more interesting than going home to another as-yet-undisclosed job. The cattle were quiet, content, and huddled together.

"Aw, you can go back if you want to," Orin told his sister. "I'll stay till noon." He didn't want to miss the fun if the skunk made another appearance.

"I don't wanna go home," Doris said when she heard about the boys' experience in the culvert.

After some discussion, Jerold said both Orin and Doris could stay. Olga had told them that whenever a decision needed to be made, the two younger kids should listen to Jerold.

"We'll take turns watching the cows, and whoever wants to can go back into the culvert where it's cool," Jerold announced.

Herding cattle wasn't nearly so boring when it was done with friends in a secret, cool, underground shelter. What had begun as drudgery had turned into quite a dangerous and exciting adventure.

After they finished the cookies and nectar, the boys began plotting a return excursion into the culvert. "I hear a car coming. Let's get into the culvert and see how much noise it makes when it drives on top of us," Orin challenged his friends.

But the fun came to an abrupt halt when Jerold hollered, "The skunk is back! Run!" The original squatter had decided to reclaim its territory, and the invaders fled as fast as their legs could carry them. The intruders wisely decided to let the skunk have its house back without a fight.

Later in the day, after Jerold, Orin, and Doris got home, Mama asked, "Did you kids see a skunk today? It sure smells skunky around here."

Jerold told Olga what had happened while they were in the culvert under the road. "It was a big skunk, too, Mama. I saw it running across the road."

Orin chimed in, "What would happen if we got sprayed?"

"You were lucky," Olga said. "Skunk spray is a dangerous poison. It really stings, and it causes blisters. If you ever get sprayed, you'll smell like a skunk for a long, long time. From now on, you kids stay out of the culverts, even if it's hot."

They weren't much interested in smelling like a skunk, so they promised to do as their mama said.

The next day, Jerold and Orin took the cows, their lunch

buckets, and water and headed for the hills in a different direction. They had little hope of finding shade on that sweltering day. Trees on the prairie were few and far between, and their most promising relief, a culvert, had been ruined forever by a small critter with a strong, stinky, stinging spray.

The Land of Make-Believe

Mud Pies

Year after year, farm families struggled to survive the severe droughts that plagued their land during the Great Depression. Due to the lack of rain, most crops failed, and the dirt turned into sand. Russian thistles were the only feed available for the cattle. Not surprisingly, many cows died. Farmers usually tried to sell their herds before this happened. Watching their bony cattle be herded one by one into trucks brought tears to the eyes of many families.

The Red Cross occasionally brought used clothing and some food for starving families. But with money so short, parents certainly couldn't afford toys for their children. So children created their own ways of entertaining themselves.

Doris became very skilled in the world of make-believe. In the summer, she spent hours working at her mud-pie stand. As she dragged boards and planks across the yard to set up a restaurant by the granary or close to the house, she imagined owning her own restaurant in town. It was not easy to find something to set the planks on to make the counters. But after searching the yard, the garage, behind the granaries, and the barn, she'd always find a small empty barrel, a couple of empty gas cans, an old cream can, or even a wood stump that would suffice. Before long, her make-believe restaurant was ready for customers. Her cafe had a different name each day. On one particular day, it was the Stop and Eat Restaurant. However, there were days when it was just a coffee shop. It all depended on how much time Doris had to play.

Many customers stopped in for the good food served at the Stop and Eat Restaurant—doughnuts, rolls, pancakes, pie, cake, cookies, and soup. Doris usually had quite a variety of selections on her handwritten menu. Customers ordered off the menu, and Doris wrote the orders on pieces of paper. Prices were reasonable, sometimes negotiable. Milk, coffee, and nectar were also served.

When a pretend customer came in, the conversation went something like this:

"Oh, hello, Alice. Is this your little girl?"

(Pause)

"How old is she?"

(Pause)

"Only three? My, she's a big girl." Doris handed the pretend Alice a menu. "We have some good bean soup today, with a ham sandwich. I only have a little left, as many have liked and ordered it. We also have chocolate cake, which is fresh out of the oven." Doris usually sold chocolate cake, as the color of the mud was much like chocolate cake.

"I'll have apple pie later this afternoon."

(Pause)

Doris brought Alice a cup of coffee in a small tin can. "What would you like to order?" she asked.

"We'll have the soup, a sandwich, and two cookies. Could

Darlene have just a small cup of soup?" Alice asked. "But I will have a bowl."

"Of course," Doris said. "I think I have enough soup left for both of you." Doris wrote the order on a piece of paper. "It will be ready in a minute."

Doris went to her "kitchen" to prepare the order. It was brought to the customer in a tin sardine can, a broken cup, and a pie plate her Mama had said she could play with. The two flattened mud pies became ham sandwiches, and the two cookies were sprinkled with cornmeal. Olga often gave Doris a small amount of flour and cornmeal for her to use in the restaurant.

Other make-believe people wandered into the popular café as well.

"Oh, hello, George. Sit down. Do you want coffee and two doughnuts?"

"Yup!" pretend George said as he sat down close to Alice. George had the same thing every day.

"Nice warm day today, huh, George?" Doris commented.

"Yep!" George said. "Sure do need some rain, though."

Doris brought pretend George his two doughnuts on a plate, along with a cup of coffee. Olga gave Doris any coffee that may have been left from breakfast in a jar or tin can.

Alice was given her bill. Ten cents for the soup, five cents for the cookies, and fifteen cents for the sandwich. She paid Doris and headed for the door.

"Good-bye, Alice. Come again," Doris said as she put the pretend money in her apron.

Later, customers walked in for fresh apple pie and coffee. Doris was busy most of the afternoon making mud-pie food and waiting on customers. Doris loved her restaurant. She made many friends, as people seemed to like her food and good service.

Her make-believe world was very real to her. She created

new foods every day, trying to make things that looked like food her mama made. Running her restaurant changed hours of boredom into hours of excitement and enjoyment. She had many loyal customers who wandered in to eat, drink coffee, or just shoot the breeze. These imaginary friends became real to her, even appearing in her dreams.

Selling Magazines

On rainy days, Doris sold magazines. She searched the house for newspapers, magazines, books, catalogs, or any other paper item she might be able to sell to a farmwife on her magazine route. She collected a tablet, a pencil, and make-believe order forms; walked to the garage; got into the car; and pretended to drive. She often ran into muddy roads. Seldom did she meet another car on the narrow road. If she did, she inched the car as close to the ditch as she dared. She drove for a while and then turned into the Strand farm.

Someone always came out of the house when the dog barked. Doris rolled down her window and greeted the pretend farm lady. "Oh, hello, Mrs. Strand," she said. "Are you having a busy day?"

Mrs. Strand said she was always busy, yet she seemed to enjoy having someone to visit with for a short time. The Strands didn't have any close neighbors or children.

"I'm selling magazines today," Doris said. "Would you like to see what I have for sale?"

Mrs. Strand smiled and said they didn't have much money, but she would look anyway.

"My prices are cheap. Besides, some are on sale. I'm sure you would enjoy reading any of these." Doris showed her a couple of magazines.

Make-believe Mrs. Strand smiled. "How nice," she said.

"Does your husband like to read?" the saleslady asked.

Mrs. Strand looked at the choices. She seemed to enjoy visiting with Doris and didn't seem in a hurry to go back into the house to finish her ironing. Many days could go by without Mrs. Strand seeing anyone but her husband.

"How much is the *Farm Weekly*?" make-believe Mrs. Strand asked. "Yes, my husband likes to read, but he doesn't have much time. He usually works from sunup to sundown."

"Oh, that's free if you order two of the others," Doris told her. (Doris had heard peddlers tell her mama that when she looked at their products.)

After looking through many of the available selections, Mrs. Strand ordered the *Ladies' Home Journal*, a paper-doll book, and the *Farm Weekly*. Doris seemed to sell products and merchandise she wished she had. She wrote out the order and gave a receipt to Mrs. Strand, who was standing by the car window. Doris told her again that the *Farm Weekly* was free because she had ordered two other items. "Your bill will come in the mail with the first magazine next month," she told Mrs. Strand.

Doris said good-bye to her make-believe customer, rolled up the window, and drove to the next farm. The same process continued until she ran out of customers, until she got tired of selling magazines, or until Mama called her to come into the house and do her chores.

Doris didn't make any real money running her businesses, but she loved driving the car by herself, even if she hadn't moved a foot; and she loved her mud-pie café, even though she never made a penny serving pie, coffee, soup, and sandwiches. She didn't mind a bit that the only thing real about her pretend businesses was all the fun she had running them.

The Little Red Wagon

"I dubs on the wagon first!" Orin yelled as he went out the door after supper on a hot summer evening.

"No, that's not fair!" Doris said. "You had it first last night. It's my turn tonight."

Jerold sided with his little sister. "She's right, Orin. You had it first last night. It's her turn tonight."

"Why do you have to stick up for her? She always gets her way."

With that, Orin went off to the other side of the house to set up his "store," while Jerold and Doris started marking out the road on the ground with sticks and stones. Almost every summer night, Doris and her brothers played Town around the house with their little red wagon. On rare occasions, if it had rained, sloshing and getting stuck in the mud made it even more fun.

Few toys in those days got more use than the little red wagon. It was top on the priority list for most families when and if money ever became available for extras. The cost of this wagon was less than five dollars, but five dollars back then was a lot of money. It bought two pairs of overalls and shirts for the boys, groceries for a week, one hundred pounds of flour, stockings and underwear for the three kids, or a pair of work shoes for John. However, the little red wagon was much more than just a favorite toy. It was used to carry heavy tools and dirt from place to place, to bring ice from the ice house to the kitchen, to haul wood into the house for the stoves, and to bring water to the garden.

Doris dreamed of having a doll buggy, but somehow she knew it would always be just a dream. Instead, she pulled her doll, Betsy, from place to place in the wagon.

When it was her turn, Doris pulled the wagon on the makeshift road in the make-believe town. Her legs were neither strong enough nor long enough to drive it like her brothers, so she pulled it instead. If she was pretending to be a customer, she was Mrs. Smestad. But when she was a storekeeper, she became Gladys. Orin often took on the character of Oscar Hoff, a farmer. Jerold liked to be the sheriff.

The town had many businesses: grocery store, general merchandise store, café, gas station, and sometimes even a jail. The imagination of the driver determined the businesses in the town on any given night. If the driver of the wagon car pulled into the store with only a make-believe storekeeper, a variety of conversations could be heard.

"I'm wondering if you have light-blue ribbon and white stockings. It's my little girl's birthday next week, and she has been wishing and hoping for white stockings," Mrs. Smestad asked.

"No," replied the make-believe storekeeper. "We won't have them until December."

"Thank you. I'll come back then," Mrs. Smestad said.

She then drove to the grocery store for a few groceries. She waited by the counter until the make-believe storekeeper was finished with Mrs. Monson.

"Oh, hello, Mrs. Smestad. It's nice to see you today," he said. "How can I help you?"

Mrs. Smestad ordered a box of oatmeal, a jar of Ovaltine, a pound of brown sugar, a small box of sugar lumps, a bar of P&G soap, two all-day suckers, and two apples. The grocery man found the groceries the on the shelves of his store and brought them to the counter. Mrs. Smestad paid her bill and put the sack of groceries in her car.

After two circles around the town, the driver's turn was up. Doris went to her store, and Orin jumped in the car. With one leg in the wagon, the other pushing on the ground, he could steer most anywhere.

"What kind of store will you have?" Orin asked Doris before he drove away.

"I have a toy store," she said, "with lots of dolls."

"Oh, for dumb! Who's ever going to stop at that? I'm sure not!"

He drove off in the opposite direction to give Doris time to fix up her store. He stopped for a minute and yelled from the car to Gladys, the pretend storekeeper. "Do you have any marbles in your store?"

Gladys told him it was only a doll store with doll buggies, doll clothes, dishes, and blankets. Doris always had a store that sold things she liked and wanted. Orin drove on, and Gladys got busy waiting on another customer.

Orin soon came to the sheriff's jailhouse. "Hey," he yelled from his car with a sly, curious grin. "Got any business?"

"Well, not yet," the sheriff said. "But I hear some lawbreakers are on the loose. They might be wandering into town later tonight."

"Boy! That could be bad," Orin-as-Oscar said.

"Yeah, but I was told the Lone Ranger and Tonto are out looking for them, too," the sheriff answered, seeming both excited and concerned.

"Ya gonna let us know if they're comin' over the hill?" Oscar asked, intrigued by the possibility that robbers might be somewhere close by.

"Oh, yeah!" the sheriff hollered back. "I'm on the lookout.

With the Lone Ranger and Tonto around, don't think we have much to worry about."

Oscar pulled away and headed down the road. "Good luck," he called back. "Better be careful."

After Orin made his two turns around the house, he got out of the car and hollered, "Your turn, Jerold!"

Orin and Jerold exchanged places. Orin became Peter, a blacksmith, and Jerold was Nils, a farmer. Nils decided he needed a few repairs for his binder,* a small doll for his little girl, and two bananas. He found everything he wanted in this busy, thriving town on the prairie.

Occasionally, Doris asked one of her brothers for a ride in the wagon. "Orin, I need to go the locker plant.† Will you give me a ride? Please?" Doris loved to be pulled on the bumpy road.

"A ride? It's not that far. You can walk." And off he went around the house. Doris was disappointed but not surprised.

When it was Jerold's turn to have the wagon, she tried her luck again. "Jerold, can I have a ride? Puh-lease?"

He started driving away and then stopped. "Oh, okay, Suzie!" he said. "Jump in. I'll pull you around once. Just once!"

It was getting dark when Olga called from the kitchen door. "It's almost dark now. You kids better go to the water tank to wash up and come in. It's bedtime."

The three siblings reluctantly parked the car and headed for the water tank to scrub off the mud. They went into the house, put their pajamas on, and crawled into bed.

"Mama, do you know what kind of store I'm going to have

---

* A machine pulled by a tractor to cut and tie grain into bundles

† A business that rented large storage compartments kept below zero to people for storing meat and other food

tomorrow night?" Doris asked her mama before she said her prayers.

"I can't imagine," Mama said.

"I'm gonna have a candy store, and suckers will be free for all the kids my age."

Mama smiled. "That will be nice," she said as she tucked the blanket around Doris. "You'll have lots of customers."

Soon Doris and her brothers were in a dream world with high mountains, lots of apples, oranges, and bananas; pretty dresses with ruffles; shiny new shoes; and all the free candy they could eat.

Ice Cream Every Summer

"John, are you saying you think we should get an icebox?" Olga was excited at the thought.

"I've been thinking how much easier it would be for you if you had a cool place to keep food. Besides, I think we might save money in the long run," John said.

"Yes, John, it would be much easier, for sure, and it would be nice to be able to store food in a cool place right in the kitchen," Olga replied. "But you have to get the ice during the winter. This is a big job. Are you sure you want to do this?"

Very few people owned an icebox in their community. It probably hinged on the fact that getting the ice during the winter was a job most husbands didn't have a mind to do.

Doris heard the conversation between her mama and daddy. As soon as John went out to do chores, she asked Olga anxiously, "Mama, are we getting an icebox?"

Mama looked at her and tried not to sound too excited. "Well, Doris, Daddy says he thinks it would be a good idea. It sure would be nice, wouldn't it?"

"Could we have ice cream then?" Doris wondered.

"It takes ice to make ice cream, and we would have ice," Olga said. "Just think–we could have the Caseys over for ice cream on a hot summer night. Wouldn't that be fun?"

Doris couldn't think of anything she'd like better.

So two more jobs were added to John's already busy week. Having an icebox required not only ice but an icehouse for storing the ice during the hot summer months. When Jerold and Orin heard about the icebox, they were almost as excited as their little sister.

"Will you boys help build the icehouse?" John asked, knowing full well what their answer would be.

It was fall, and most of the harvesting was finished. School had started, but the very next Saturday, John and the boys started the icehouse project. With shovels in hand, Jerold and Orin helped their daddy decide where the icehouse should be built. They started digging a short distance from the house. John used a Fresno dirt scraper* pulled by his two horses to make a deep pit, while the boys shoveled out the extra dirt.

"Daddy," Jerold asked, "can I run the scraper?"

"No, Jerold, it's a heavy job. Maybe when you get older and a little bigger."

Jerold was content with the answer, but he was anxious to try. He seemed sure he could drive the horses and run the scraper at the same time. Orin seemed satisfied with shoveling dirt.

By suppertime, the pit was deep enough to suit John. The boys put their shovels back in the shed and ran to the house. John unhitched the horses, and soon the family sat down for supper. "The boys really worked hard today, Olga. Think they deserve an extra piece of apple pie."

The next day, John, with the help of his sons, built a hip roof over the pit from scrap lumber and then covered it with straw. A small entrance on the north side enabled a person to go inside to retrieve ice. "The easiest job is almost done, boys," John said to Orin and Gerald. "Next we have to get the ice, but we have a few more months to worry about that."

"When will we get the new icebox?" Doris kept asking. She had little understanding of how much work was involved to make this dream come true.

---

* A piece of equipment pulled by horses to dig and haul dirt

“Don’t get too anxious, Doris. It will be after Christmas. Daddy has to wait until the river freezes before he can get ice.”

“When is Christmas, Mama?”

“Well, this is September, then it’s October, November, and December.”

It was too long to wait, and Doris went out to swing.

The Sanish Excursion

In late January, John was in town playing cards for the afternoon with some of his friends when he thought to ask his neighbor about going to Sanish* with him for a truckload of ice.

“Say, Orville,” he asked. Orville was his partner in whist.† “I plan to go to the river for some ice. Was wonderin’, if you aren’t busy on Friday, if you’d help me out. It’s been pretty cold; the river should be frozen by now.”

It didn’t take Orville long to think about it. “Ya, sure, John,

---

* A small town close to the river

† A popular card game

I'll go. Be kinda fun to get away from the missus for a day," he said with a grin. "Should be worth a dish or two of ice cream next summer, eh?"

John readily agreed. He then asked Olga's brother-in-law, Philmor, to join the effort.

The next Friday, Philmor and Orville met at John's place, and the three started out for Sanish early in the morning. It was cold and blustery, with the wind blowing loose snow across the road. Olga had packed a sack of lunch for each of the men. She was more than willing to do anything she could to get an icebox by summer.

It took more than an hour to get to Sanish. Once they reached the riverbank, John parked the truck on the river, hoping the crew who cut the ice would not be late. The two ice cutters were waiting. They walked over to shake the hands of the two men.

"You must be John," one of them said.

"Ya, and these two guys, Philmor and Orville, are along to help."

Huge chunks, twelve to fourteen inches square, were cut by local men with ice-cutting equipment. John, Philmor, and Orville then carried them to the truck. It was heavy, exhausting work. When the sun was high in the sky, John decided it was time to see what Olga had put in the brown paper sacks. All three men scrambled into the cab, happy to be out of the freezing cold for a brief time. John had brought a thermos of coffee and handed a steaming hot cup to Philmor.

"Oh, boy, this is going to feel good!" he said gratefully.

After pouring two more cups, John opened his sack.

"Not sure what Olga stuck in here, but whatever it is, I don't think it's poisoned," he joked. "She's pretty anxious to fill that icehouse with ice."

Stories and jokes were exchanged as they ate roast-beef

sandwiches and doughnuts. After the last drop of coffee was gone, John hesitantly declared, "Well, we better get out there so we can finish before dark. That sun goes down pretty early these days, and I'm not sure how good the lights are on the truck."

John figured they had about seventy good-sized cubes of ice when the last chunk was wedged in. *Enough to get through the summer if we're careful,* he calculated.

"Don't think we have to worry about them melting," Orville commented as took his gloves off to warm his fingers. "I think both my hands are frozen."

"I'm not as worried about my fingers as my toes. I can't feel a thing," Philmor said.

Neither John nor Orville gave him much sympathy. Their toes were numb as well.

Now to start the truck, John thought privately. *I better try to start it before these ice cutters leave, just in case.* "Jump in, Philmor," he said. "It's going to get dark pretty soon."

Orville pushed against Philmor as hard as he could to get the door shut.

"Think you better go on a diet, Philmor," Orville teased.

"What's a diet?" Philmor asked.

On the first try, the motor on the truck just gave a soft groan. Orville and Philmor looked concerned. John tried again. No luck. If he flooded the engine, he knew he'd be in big trouble. "C'mon, Bessie," John murmured. On the third try, the motor finally turned over. The men sighed in relief.

Now John's only concern was having enough gas to get home. "It always takes more gas when you got a load and when it's this cold. I hope you guys have enough steam left to push in case we run out," he added.

Both men remained silent. They thought John was kidding—at least, they hoped he was.

Jerold and Orin eagerly awaited the sound and the lights of the approaching truck. When they heard it roll into the yard, they grabbed their coats, caps, and mittens and raced to the icehouse. There wasn't much haggling about helping. They, too, had the wonderful vision of making and enjoying ice cream on hot summer days.

John backed the truck up to the icehouse, while Orville and the boys jumped into the pit. It was not an easy task unloading the large chunks and arranging them in layers. Jerold and Orin stood ready with shovels to cover the layers with coal slack,* then straw. It took over an hour to finish the backbreaking job.

When they were done, John asked, "Well, how much do I owe you two guys for today? It was a pretty hard day's work."

Neither one wanted to respond. During the Depression,

* Finely grated coal, like sand

people didn't expect much pay for helping one another. Extending a hand whenever asked was a way of life.

"Oh, I'll just take a couple of dishes of ice cream next summer when it's hotter than blazes," Orville answered.

Philmor said nothing. He was John's brother-in-law, and John had already helped him out many times. However, Philmor didn't have a job, he had five kids to feed, and he was always in need of cash. John handed him three dollars. "Thanks, John. I sure can use it," Philmor replied, grateful for John's generosity.

"I think Olga has supper ready for us. Let's go in and warm up. The boys will finish the job."

Olga had made meatballs and gravy with mashed potatoes, two pies, and homemade bread with fresh butter. She also opened two jars of corn she had canned from her garden. By the time the three men, Jerold, and Orin had heaped their plates with their favorite foods, there was barely enough left in the bowls for Olga and Doris.

"*Tusen takk*, Olga. That was sure good," Philmor commented as he tipped back in his chair. "This hot coffee has thawed out my toes, too, I think."

The mood, even though all of them were worn out from the long, hard day, was jovial. They talked about the day for a short time, and then Orville decided to head to his house, which was across the road a short distance from John's. Olga asked Philmor to stay overnight; she knew he shouldn't be driving his old car home after dark.

Summer Time

Having ice during the hot summers meant not only eating ice cream often but having chilled milk to drink, whipped cream on Jell-O, and cold nectar. Meat was safely stored, butter tasted good all week, and eggs never spoiled.

Olga found other benefits, too. As the ice melted, it drained into a pan under the icebox. She used this soft water to water plants, take a sponge bath,* or shampoo her hair. None of the kids objected to pulling the little red wagon to the icehouse for ice when Olga needed it. Since it was such a cool retreat from a hot summer day, they often lingered in the icehouse for a while before returning with the requested ice.

The icehouse also became a lookout station for hawks as they swooped into the yard, picking up baby chicks. Jerold, being the oldest, was the only one allowed to shoot the gun that was kept in the pit.

"Golly, Mama," Orin often complained, "I'm almost as old as Jerold. It's not fair. I should be able to watch once in a while."

His complaining didn't change Olga's mind. It was not only that Jerold was older; she wanted to avoid any fighting between the boys. She explained the danger of guns and that she and John only wanted one in charge of the weapon. But as soon as Olga had explained this to Orin, she saw a hawk swooping across the yard.

"Hawk! Hawk!" Olga hollered as she ran out the door.

Jerold ran as fast as he could to the icehouse. He aimed the gun and pulled the trigger as the hawk was flying away with a chick in its claws. But he missed.

Everyone was told to watch for hawks. Jerold spent a lot of time in the cool ice pit. He wanted to keep an eye out for hawks, but it was also a wonderful way to get out of the sweltering sun.

---

* When water was scarce, people washed from head to toe using a cloth, soap, and a small amount of water in a basin.

Orin wondered if he would get a turn next summer, when he would be the same age Jerold was now. There was no one to play with when Jerold was in the icehouse. Many times, he crawled in, too, just to get away from the sun and Doris—and he secretly hoped Jerold might let him take a shot. Jerold knew better and told his brother not to keep asking.

Having an icebox was indeed a good thing. Once Olga, Doris, Orin, and Jerold got used to having cold milk, cool drinks, and whipped cream on Jell-O, they were sure they could not live without it. And few neighbors refused the invitation to come over for some ice cream and cookies on a hot summer night.

"Mama, can we have Caseys over for ice cream after supper?" Doris asked.

"That's a good idea Doris. Why don't you run over and ask them?" Olga said.

Doris was out the door before Olga finished talking. *Yes,* Doris thought as she ran down the road. *The ice box is a good thing. A really good thing.*

“Jerold! The House Is Locked!”

“John, we better get going early in the morning so we are back by the time the children get home from school,” Olga told her husband before they went to bed. John and Olga had planned to go to a neighboring town the next day to do some shopping, buy supplies for some repairs, and have new soles put on John’s only pair of shoes. Olga had managed to save a few cents from cream checks* for her own spending money and was anxious to look at things in different stores. Her two dollars could buy any number of items she liked.

The school bus dropped Jerold, Orin, and Doris off at the mailbox around four o’clock. They raced to the house, knowing that Mama would have fresh bread, doughnuts, or cookies waiting for them. Olga seldom disappointed her three small children.

Orin got to the door first. He turned the knob, but, for some reason, it wouldn’t open. He tried and tried, but the door wouldn’t budge. “Jerold,” he yelled, “the door won’t open. Something’s wrong.”

“Let me try,” Jerold said, thinking Orin had not turned it hard enough. Jerold tried three times, turning and twisting the knob, but it still wouldn’t open. It *was* locked! *But it’s never, ever been locked before,* he muttered to himself.

“Let’s knock on the window,” Orin suggested. “Maybe Mama is taking a nap.”

---

* Cream checks: Money families earned from selling cream

So Jerold began rapping on the window. "Mama!" he called. "Maaa-maa!" He yelled louder and kept knocking. Still no answer. Orin ran to the shed to see if the car was gone.

"Jerold, the car isn't there. They've gone somewhere."

Doris began to cry. It was cold and windy, and she was shivering. She was petrified that someone might be hiding in the house—a tramp or a burglar or some mean man. "Where are they? Where is Mama, Jerold?" she asked frantically.

"I don't know, Doris. They've gone somewhere. I'm sure they'll be back any minute," he added. He was trying to reassure his little sister that nothing bad had happened, even though he realized it was very strange that his mama and daddy had left without telling him.

The two brothers were scared, too, but they tried not to show it.

Jerold took charge. They waited out in the cold wind for a little while, hoping to see the car coming down the road.

"Come on, sis. Let's go wait in the brooder house, out of the wind. It will be warmer in there." Jerold took his little sister by the hand and began walking across the yard.

"What if something bad has happened to Mama and Daddy?" Doris sobbed. "What if we never see them again? What's gonna happen to us?"

"Don't worry, sis," Jerold consoled. "They'll be back before dark. Maybe they had car trouble or a flat tire."

Doris stopped crying. But she could not stop being scared to death. She couldn't stop thinking about a burglar hiding in the closet or under the bed. Or what could've happened to her mama and daddy.

They stayed in the brooder house, listening and waiting for the sound of the car driving into the yard. Five minutes seemed like an hour. Twenty minutes went by. Then forty-five. Still no sign of Mama and Daddy. And it was starting to get dark. Even Jerold was getting worried. Doris kept fussing and crying.

"I know something bad has happened! I just know it! They never leave us alone. We'll never see them again!" Big tears were rolling down her cheeks.

"Oh, quit being such a bawl baby, Doris," Orin said, trying to cover up his own fear.

The sky was getting darker and darker. Jerold had decided

that if Mama and Daddy had not come home by dark, they would walk over to the Caseys' place half a mile away. He waited a few more minutes before he said, "Come on, sis. We're going to walk over to the Caseys' and wait."

Orin was already heading for the road when he heard the sound of a distant car. He turned to look. "There they are!" he yelled. "They're coming down the road!"

Jerold and Doris stood by the kitchen door, watching the car drive into the yard. John and Olga could not figure out what was going on.

"Why aren't the kids in the house, John?" Olga asked. "Something must be wrong!"

John didn't have an answer. He stopped the car and quickly got out.

"Mama! Mama! The house is locked, and we couldn't get in. We had to stand in the brooder house and wait!" Doris said as she ran to Olga, shivering and sobbing.

"Yeah, and she's been cryin' for an hour!" Orin chimed in.

Olga hugged and held Doris while the two boys watched their dad try to open the door. He turned and twisted the knob just like the boys had done, but it was locked tight. *How could this happen?* he wondered. *It must've locked when I slammed it shut.*

He went to the garage to get some tools and soon had the door pried open. All five of them hurried into the cold house. Olga quickly threw some kindling into the stove. Before long, the house was warm, and Olga started cooking supper. Doris stood by the half-open oven door, still shivering, more from being scared than from being cold.

Doris soon began smiling when Olga told her what she had seen and bought in the department store in Plaza. Jerold and Orin tried to hide their fear by acting as if nothing much had happened. But Doris still didn't understand why her mama and daddy hadn't been home when they returned from school and why the door was locked. "Why weren't you home, Mama? We were all really, really scared something bad had happened to you."

"Oh, I know," Olga said, "and I'm really sorry that you got so frightened and cold, Doris. But Daddy had to wait for his repairs longer than he planned, and once it started getting dark, we couldn't drive very fast. I never, ever thought the door could be locked and you couldn't get in the house. That's never happened before."

Soon the house was warm, and Olga had supper on the table. The three kids were hungry and ate all of their potatoes, meat, and corn. Olga opened a jar of peach sauce she had canned as an extra treat.

By eight o'clock, Doris, Orin, and Jerold were tucked into bed.

"We will *always* check the door if we have to be gone when you come home from school," Olga promised her three kids.

Doris felt safe. She had looked again to make sure there wasn't a bad guy under her bed. She and her doll, Betsy, were soon asleep.

John and Olga sat by the potbelly stove and listened to the radio for a while before going to bed. They both were very thankful that their three little kids were safe and sound and asleep.

The family learned three lessons from this experience: Mama and Daddy should always check the door before they leave; the children should go to the neighbors for help in an emergency; and Doris should always listen to her older brothers in times of trouble.

The frightful day was over but not soon forgotten by John, Olga, Jerold, Orin, and especially Doris, who was very relieved no one was hiding in the closet or under her bed.

“But Mama! I Don’t Wanna Go to School!”

Everyone on the farm worked from sunup to sunset almost every day during the summer. Even five-year-old Doris had chores to do. She helped Mama take care of the garden, wash clothes every Monday, wipe dishes, clean the separator, and sometimes she helped clean the house. But the family also had a lot of fun during the summer. They went to town celebrations and the fair, made ice cream, had frequent picnics, and went to town every Saturday night.

But now it was September, and summer was over. It was time for Olga to remind her three children that school would be starting in a few days.

“But I don’t wanna go to school, Mama!” Doris said. “I don’t know any of the town kids, and I’m scared. Please don’t make me go, Mama! Pleeeeeeease!” Doris begged.

Olga looked at her little girl. “But Doris,” Olga said as she pulled Doris onto her lap, “everyone has to go to school. It’s the rule.”

Doris began sobbing. “But what if no one likes me and someone teases me because I’m from the country?”

"That won't happen," Olga assured her frightened first grader. "Besides, Orin and Jerold will be with you."

Doris couldn't stop crying. Tears ran down her cheeks, and her sobbing turned into short, choking sniffles. Olga told Doris how lonely she would be when she was gone. "I'll be alone all day, and I will miss you, Doris," she said. "I'm not used to being alone. Promise me you will come home every day as quickly as you can."

This made Doris feel better, like she was important. "Oh, I promise, Mama. I promise!"

The morning of the first day of school, Olga woke the boys and Doris earlier than usual to allow plenty of time for getting ready.

"Is it already time to wake up?" Doris asked when Olga gently nudged her. "I wasn't done sleeping yet."

Doris got up, washed her face and hands, and ate breakfast. She went to her cot in the corner and looked at the dress Mama had sewn for her first day of school. It was a blue dress with short, puffy sleeves and matching ribbon around the neck. Olga had saved money all summer to buy the blue material. She wanted Doris to feel good and look nice on her first day.

"Oh, how cute you look!" Olga exclaimed. "The dress makes you look so special."

Doris was proud of her new dress. She hadn't had a brand-new dress for a long time. Olga brushed Doris's hair and tied a blue ribbon around a few of the curls she had made the night before with a curling iron.*

Suddenly, Doris thought about getting on the bus, and her eyes filled with tears. "Mama, do I have to go into the room all by myself?" she asked, her voice quivering.

"Oh, no, Doris. You will be with Orin and Jerold. They both

---

* Iron heated in the chimney of a kerosene lamp.

love school, and you will, too." Olga then turned to Jerold, a third-grader, and motioned for him to tell his little sister how much fun school was.

"Ah . . . Yeah, Suzie," he said, using his pet name for his sister. "School is lots of fun. But I was scared, too, when I started first grade. And I could *only* talk Norwegian."

"Yes, I know, Jerold," Olga agreed. "You were very brave."

After listening to his little sister, Orin finally chimed in. "Oh, quit being such a big baby, Doris. I didn't cry last year."

"Yeah, but you had Jerold, and I don't have a sister," Doris reminded him.

"You and Orin must help your sister today," Olga told the boys. "She is afraid, because she doesn't know anyone. Jerold, you make sure she finds the first-grade room."

"Okay, Mama," Jerold promised.

Doris tied her shoes and started putting her school supplies in her bag, including a box of eight new crayons, a tablet, and a pencil. She had kept them under her pillow so her brothers wouldn't find them. She heard the roar of the school bus coming down the road, and panic set in again. "Is the bus here, Mama?" she asked, choking back tears.

Olga gave Doris a big hug. "It's here, Doris. It's time for you to go."

Jerold took his little sister's hand and headed for the road. Doris looked back and saw Olga waving from the door, then Jerold helped her climb up the high step into the bus.

The three Hermundstad kids were always the first ones on the bus and the last ones off, because Orville, the bus driver, lived right across the road.

"So you're starting school today, Doris," Orville said, not realizing how frightened Doris was.

Doris did not answer. She only held Jerold's hand tighter.

Doris had never seen the inside of the bus. Orville had built a box on the back end of his truck. It had small windows on the door and on one side. There were benches on all sides and one in the center. Doris felt safe sitting between her brothers.

Now it was Olga's turn to shed a tear as she waved one last time to her kids. After the bus drove away, she went into the empty house and called her neighbor Myrt.

"Myrt," she said, "Doris just went to school, and I'm alone. It's a very strange feeling. Can you walk over for a cup of coffee?"

Myrt, who was scrubbing her kitchen floor, readily agreed. "I'll be over in five minutes," she said. The two farms were just a stone's throw apart. One could almost holler from the mailbox to the other farm.

An hour later, the bus was filled with twenty students from age five to seventeen. Finally it arrived at the schoolhouse. "Everybody out!" Orville yelled as he slid the window open between the cab and the bus. "Take it easy!" he told the older boys, who were shoving and pushing. "There are some little kids on the bus."

As they hurried into schoolhouse, Jerold took Doris by her hand. "I'll show you where your room is."

Orin ran ahead, eager to see where he would be sitting in the second grade.

Miss Kelly, the first-grade teacher, came to the door and noticed Jerold holding his sister's hand as he led her into the room. "Oh, what a nice big brother," she told Jerold. Then she put her arm around Doris and told Jerold he could leave.

The room was full of strange faces. Doris knew they were all staring at her, even though she was not looking up. As Miss Kelly showed her where to sit, she noticed a big teardrop on Doris' cheek and realized how frightened she must be. "Your name is Doris, isn't it?" she asked as she sat down and put

Doris on her lap. Doris hung her head and nodded. “Don’t be afraid,” Miss Kelly said. “You are very safe in my room. We will be learning many new things, and soon you will have lots of new friends.”

After a few minutes, Doris was ready to go to her desk.

Miss Kelly told the class that Doris was afraid because she didn't have any town friends. Everyone was looking at her, and Doris wanted to run out the door, down the stairs, and outside where no one could find her. But she didn't. She stayed. Soon the tears dried up, and she began looking around the room. She liked what she saw. There were lots of books on the shelves and the biggest chalkboard she'd ever seen. ABC pictures decorated the wall, and by the window she saw a large sandbox. This was something new to Doris, and Olga had not told her about it. How exciting!

Doris discovered that all the faces she thought had been staring at her had names. Miss Kelly called them one by one, and each had to stand when his or her name was called. Doris was the second to last. When Miss Kelly finally said her name, she stood up and tried to smile.

The class of first-graders looked at books, drew pictures, and colored—all the things Doris loved to do. The class took turns playing in the sandbox, and before Doris could even think about being scared, it was time for lunch. After lunch, it was Doris's turn to play in the sandbox with a girl named Donna Mae.

When the bell rang, signaling the end of the first day of school, Miss Kelly asked the class to stand in a row and march out together. Jerold was waiting for his little sister in the hallway. Miss Kelly said good-bye to the children. "I will be very excited to see all of you tomorrow," she said.

Miss Kelly was the prettiest lady Doris had ever seen. She had long red fingernails, red lipstick, and even red hair, almost the same color as hers, just like Mama had said. Doris was excited to come back the next day, too.

When she got home, Doris told Olga all about her classroom,

her new friends, and what Miss Kelly had them do. “And Mama! I got to draw pictures and color. And I even played in the sandbox! It was fun, Mama. I like school!”

“I knew you would,” Olga answered. “But you know what? I was really, really lonesome here all myself. I finally had to call Myrt to come over for coffee.”

Doris smiled and felt special. Very special.

An Early Morning Sleigh Ride

Olga heard the clock strike five. She crawled out of bed, slipped on John's wool shirt and warm socks, and threw a wool blanket around her shoulders. It was still very dark—and cold! She found her way into the kitchen and lit the kerosene lamp. John had been up earlier to stoke the two stoves. Heavy frost covered all the windows, which told Olga it was cold outside, blisteringly cold.

She noticed that the water in the pitcher on the washstand had a thin layer of ice on it. She scraped frost off the window and checked the thermometer. "John," she said as she shook him out of a deep sleep, "It's twenty-eight below! Do you think we should send the kids today?"

"Send 'em, Olga. They'll make it."

Olga put more wood and a couple of small chunks of coal in the stove before she woke Jerold and Orin. The teakettle was always full of water on the front of the stove. Once it became hot, Olga simply kept replenishing what she used. She felt the water in the reservoir of the stove, hoping it might be lukewarm. It wasn't! But the kids were used to washing their faces in ice-cold water in the morning.

Mornings meant getting the three little kids out of bed,

getting them dressed and fed, and making lunches before six. Since they lived across the road from the bus driver, the Hermundstad kids were the first ones on in the morning and the last ones off at night. Jerold, Orin, and Doris spent six hours getting to and from school every day during the winter.

"Bring your clothes and dress here by the stove where it's warmer," she told Jerold and Orin. "Be sure to wear your heavy shirts and a wool sweater."

Olga woke Doris and told her she had to hurry. "Orville will soon be here, and I want you all to eat a bowl of hot oatmeal before you leave."

"Mama, is it cold?"

"Yes, Doris. It's very cold. You have to wear your long underwear, brown stockings, the long-sleeved dress I made for you, and the sweater from Grandma."

A few minutes before six, the three kids were bundled up in their heavy jackets, scarves, caps, snow pants, and buckle overshoes.* Olga sent two lunches plus an extra sack with doughnuts and cookies with each of them.

When Orville pulled up with the team and sleigh, Jerold, Orin, and Doris ran out the door and climbed into the bus as fast as they could.

"You little kids sit here close to the stove," Orville said as he headed down the field to the Caseys'. "Be careful, though, so you don't fall against it and get burned."

The school-bus sleigh, an oblong box, was built on ski-shaped runners and pulled by a team of horses. Benches were built in along the sides, and a piece of celluloid served as a window up front. Orville sat outside on a bench, driving the team. He could keep his eye on activities in the bus through the

---

* A high rubber boot worn over shoes, which snapped shut with buckles

makeshift window and yell at unruly passengers, if necessary. Teasing, joking, and laughing by the older boys kept everyone either entertained or bawling. Some kids were teased and bullied mercilessly. One older boy yelled, "John Milton Cuddles Gummer. Couldn't make 'em any dumber." Jerold, Orin and Doris were called Popeye, Wimpy and Olive Oyl. Others were accused of smelling like manure and peanut butter, while some were made fun of for wearing patched clothing.

Orville cut across the fields to shorten the trip. The drifts were deep, but the horses managed to get through them without getting stuck, which was Orville's worst nightmare. He sometimes told the older boys to get out and run for a while. He wanted to both keep them warm and give the horses a lighter load. The little kids sitting close to the stove were Doris and her friend Catherine. Despite their prime position, their bread was already half-frozen, and when they put it on the red-hot stove, the outside burned while the inside stayed ice-cold. By the time the six Maurer kids got on at the last stop, there was standing-room only on the sleigh bus.

Around ten o'clock, the bus pulled up to the schoolhouse on the edge of town. Orville got out and helped the little kids off the sleigh. "Is everybody okay?" he asked, realizing that it had been more than three hours since the Casey and Hermundstad kids had left home.

Doris and Catherine jumped off together and raced to the door. Orville told everyone he would be back around 2:30. "Tell your teachers you have to leave early."

They all ran up the stairs to their rooms, where their teachers were anxiously waiting for them. They were very relieved each day to hear the noise of the country kids in the hallways an hour after school had started.

"The country kids are here!" the town kids cheered as they entered their classroom. The town kids seemed a bit envious of the country kids, because they got to ride on a sleigh to school every day. At two thirty, before school was officially dismissed, the country kids were waiting for Orville to take them home.

The Maurer kids were dropped off first, then the three Hoffs, Johnny and Louise Havilis, the three Gummer boys, Carl Jordet, the Casey kids, and, lastly, Jerold, Orin, and Doris.

Olga was watching and waiting for them. It was almost six when she saw the team and sleigh turn into their approach. As they came in the door, all three were talking at once.

"Mama, I tried to toast my bread, but it burned," Doris said.

Orin said Doris almost started to cry once because she said she was cold. Jerold was busy petting Lady, who seemed as happy to see them as Olga.

"Did Orville have any trouble today?" she asked Jerold.

"No, but the snow is really deep. I thought the horses were going to get stuck. It was up to their bellies, but Orville kept yelling and whipping them so they wouldn't stop."

"Orville said Catherine and I could come up front and watch from the window," Doris told her mama.

"Well, I sure am glad you're home safe again. You are really tough little farm kids," she told them with a proud smile. Each day was the same for Olga. She worried about them from the time she saw them get on the sleigh in the morning until they jumped off at night. "Supper's ready, and I bet you three are hungry."

Olga tried to fix suppers she knew Jerold, Orin, and Doris liked—meatballs, gravy, mashed potatoes, corn, and fresh bread. John listened to Orin and Jerold talk about the deep snow in the fields.

"Did the horses ever stop?" He was clearly as concerned as his wife about the kids but certainly didn't want to show or admit it.

"Well," Jerold said, "he had to whip 'em pretty hard to keep them going. What would happen if the horses stopped, Daddy?" he asked.

John hesitated briefly before answering. "Well, a person can always go out and lead them through the snow, if it's real deep."

Olga waited to wash the supper dishes until the kids were in bed. They had such little time during the winter months to be together; she'd rather spend time reading a couple of stories than doing dishes.

By seven o'clock, pajamas were on, and the kids were ready for bed with no complaining. Olga made hot cocoa and gave them each a cookie while she read "Goldilocks and the Three Bears." She told each of them to give Daddy a hug before she tucked them into bed.

"John," Olga asked. "Are the kids learning as much as the town kids when they are missing so much time in the classroom?"

"More," John replied without hesitation.

The house was once again quiet like it had been all day. But this was a different kind of quiet. Olga, more than once, got up from her chair by the stove, where she was embroidering a pillowcase, to walk to the beds of Jerold, Orin, and Doris just to look at them. She was happy and very thankful to have them safely snuggled into bed for another night.

Best Friend Betsy

Doris had two brothers and no sisters. Her doll, Betsy, was her best friend. Doris fed her, rocked her, and took her everywhere. But poor Betsy was naked for a long time. Olga did not have time to sew doll clothes; besides, she didn't have many scraps from which to sew Betsy a dress. To keep Betsy warm when it was cold, Doris often asked Mama if she could use a small towel or pillowcase. Olga always said yes. During the summer, when it was hot, Betsy remained naked.

Doris longed for clothes for her doll—a dress, bloomers, a coat, and a cap. Having something to put on Betsy made playing house so much more fun.

Doris played house in the Little Red House, which sometimes was used as a chicken coop, or in the brooder house. Both places always needed cleaning when they were not in use. On the days Doris decided to play house, she took the broom and swept the feathers and chicken droppings from the floor.

Doris talked to her doll much like her mother talked to her. "Now, Betsy! You know you have to eat your food so you will get strong."

Betsy seldom argued with her mama. Olga had given Doris a small spoon and a cracked cup to use in her "house." Betsy was fed soup, potatoes, rice pudding, and canned corn.

When the boys were not using the little red wagon for chores, Doris put Betsy in the wagon and took her to different places around the farm for groceries and other supplies for her house. Doris always bought clothes for Betsy, a candy bar, new shoes, long white stockings, bananas, and some oranges in the pretend stores. Betsy always received all the things Doris wished she had. When they got back to their house, Doris dressed Betsy in her new clothes, gave her a treat, and showed her the new stockings she could wear to church on Sunday.

One wintry Saturday afternoon, Doris went to town with Olga and John while Jerold and Orin stayed home to tend the fires.

"Jerold, you watch the stovepipes for sparks. Don't let the fire get too low, but if it gets too hot, you know that sparks go up the chimney and could start a fire."

"I know, Mama. We'll be careful." Jerold had been told this many times.

"You remember what to do if that happens, don't you?"

"I know, Mama, I know," Jerold replied. "I'll throw soda in the stovepipe."

The wind was making small pillow-drifts on the road as they drove to town.

"We better not stay in town too long today, John. I'm concerned about the boys being home alone with the stoves and this wind."

"Oh, they'll be fine, Olga. It's good for them to take some responsibility. We'll be home before dark." John was looking forward to playing a couple of games of whist in the pool hall, where all the men congregated while the womenfolk shopped and visited.

The roads were heavy with snowdrifts as John, Olga, and Doris headed for home.

"We should've left earlier, John."

"We'll make it, but I'm glad we started while it's still daylight." He saw a big drift ahead and stepped on the gas. "Hang on!" he warned as he plowed through the heavy drift.

Both Doris and John laughed as they slipped from side to side on the road, but Olga saw little humor in the situation.

The boys had lit the kerosene lamp in the kitchen, so there was a dim light in the window as they drove into the yard.

"Well, the house is still standing," John teased as he stopped the car. Olga gave Doris a couple of sacks to carry in.

"What did you buy us?" Orin wanted to know as soon as Doris came in.

Olga handed them each a box of Cracker Jack. "Oh, boy!" Orin said.

"Save it until after supper, Orin," Olga told him. "Then you can open it. Did you have any trouble with the stoves?"

"Nope," Jerold said.

Both of the boys had agreed that they would not say anything about the small sparks they had seen in the kitchen chimney.

Doris walked to her cot in the corner to get Betsy. She uncovered her, but as she attempted to pick her up, she fell apart. Her arms and legs and head were still on the bed. "Mama!" she screamed. "Mama! Come here! Quick! My doll is broken! She's all in pieces!" Doris was hysterical.

Olga hurried to the corner and saw Doris holding one piece of her doll.

"See! See! They broke my doll!" she kept screaming. "Jerold and Orin broke my doll!"

Olga tried to comfort her. "Don't worry, Doris. I know Daddy can fix it," she said. She turned to the boys. "What were you and Orin doing with Doris's doll?" Olga asked Jerold.

The two brothers tried to explain what had actually happened. "Well," Jerold stuttered, "we didn't do anything. We, uh, just picked it up to see how the legs moved, and it fell apart."

"They had no business touching my doll," Doris wailed. "She's mine, and I don't touch their stuff."

When John came in and heard the commotion, he told the boys to apologize to their sister. "You boys had no business monkeying around with her doll."

"I can fix Betsy," he assured Doris. "I just have to find a long rubber band. I think I have one in the garage."

John very seldom threw anything away. He couldn't find a long rubber band, so he improvised and cut a band from an old rubber tire tube. Luck was on his side, as it turned out to be just about the right size to fix Betsy's broken body.

Before bedtime, Doris held her doll, now all in one piece. Her brothers told her they were sorry and promised they would never touch Betsy again. To make Doris feel better, Olga promised she would try to find some scraps of material and sew an outfit for Betsy next week. “Maybe Grandma has some material I can use,” she added.

Doris had decided not to try to ruin something her brothers really liked to get even. Her daddy convinced her that it was an accident and that her doll maybe would’ve broken soon anyway, because rubber bands, when stretched, get weak and break. “Betsy has a new band now,” he told Doris. “She’ll be fine for a long time.”

Doris sat on her daddy’s lap and shared an apple with him before bedtime. Without talking about it, both John and Doris understood that her brothers hadn’t meant to break her doll. Doris was very thrilled that her daddy was able to fix almost anything, even Betsy.

Daddies are special, she thought as she drifted off to sleep that night. She had even decided her brothers were okay; if they left her stuff alone, she’d leave their stuff alone. Before long, Doris and Betsy were off in dreamland, where it was Christmastime. Betsy was dressed in a pretty red velvet dress with a matching coat, and they were waiting for Santa to come with lots of presents.

Christmas on the Farm

It was December. The air was crispy cold, the ditches were filled with snow, and heavy frost covered the windows every morning. Orin, Doris, and Jerold loved jumping in the deep, snow-filled ditches. It was fun to see who jumped the deepest.

Olga looked at the calendar and suddenly realized that only a few days remained until Christmas Eve. She worried that there wouldn't be any presents under the tree for the kids. "John," she asked when he came in with more wood, "will there be any money for presents for the children?"

John had been expecting that question. He had been trying to think of what they could do and what he should tell her. For the past few years, the family had barely had enough money for food. The Red Cross sent $10 to families in dire need and brought in used clothing for families like John's. However, Olga was not aware that John had written to his sister in Fargo, asking for a loan to cover the cost of seed for spring planting. With three kids, John didn't think Olga needed more to worry about. Besides, Olga's mind, he knew, was on Christmas, not on spring seeding.

DECEMBER

"Maybe you could sew something for Doris," John suggested as he hung up his heavy canvas jacket and cap. "And I might be able to find a few scraps of lumber to make the boys a toy."

"But John," Olga replied, "that would not be special. Christmas is a special time." Uncertain, she looked away and wiped a tear from her cheek. "I was hoping we could buy something *new*. It doesn't have to be much. But there *has* to be a present under the tree for each of them," she insisted. Because they were poor and struggling like all of their neighbors, Jerold, Orin, and Doris never found more than one present with their name on it under the Christmas tree.

John hated to disappoint his wife, or his kids. But he just didn't dare spend any money during the cold winter for things they didn't really need.

Olga kept hoping and thinking. She had seen some doll things for about thirty-five cents in the hardware store in town. Olga knew Doris would love doll stuff. She played house every day with her only doll, Betsy. *Maybe I can save enough cream to make a pound of butter*, she thought. She was quite sure the grocery man would pay her at least a quarter for butter made from grade A cream. Most of their cream was sent to the Mandan Creamery every week by train, but Olga secretly decided to save half a gallon and churn it into butter, sweet cream butter. The town folk liked to buy fresh butter from the farmers.

That still left Jerold and Orin without presents. Olga kept hoping something would turn up and tried to put it out of her mind.

People raising families during the Great Depression learned to be hopeful. They never gave up. Olga heard the clock strike twelve before she finally fell asleep that night. Thoughts of what she could get the kids for Christmas kept going through her mind.

A Surprise Visitor

A couple of days later, Uncle Genald, Olga's brother, dropped in for an unexpected visit. Uncle Genald was a tall, lanky man who always wore bib overalls with both pant legs rolled up a couple of turns and a red farmer's handkerchief sticking out of the hind pocket. He seldom took his cap off, even in the house. The toes of his shoes often had holes in them.

Doris and her brothers liked Uncle Genald. He told jokes and stories that made them laugh. When it was nice outside, Uncle Genald, Jerold, and Orin played catch while Doris watched from her swing, singing as she sailed high into the clouds.

Olga and the kids were thrilled to see Uncle Genald. Olga gave him a cup of coffee and a piece of bread covered with butter and sugar. She sat down to visit with her brother, even though she had lots of things to do.

"How's Grandma?" she asked, referring to her own mother.

"She's busier than ever, trying to get all the work done every day besides doing extra baking for Christmas. Yesterday, she made *lefse*.[*] Today I think she's going to make flatbread[†] and *fattimand*."[‡]

Genald lived with his parents on the farm where Olga had grown up. Their father, Oluf, didn't do much work anymore. Doris always thought of her grandpa as very, very old.

When Uncle Genald finished his coffee, he took something out of his pocket and gave it to his sister. "Here, Olga. Go buy something for the kids." It was a dollar bill. "They have to have some special treats at Christmastime," he said. "Maybe they'd like a box of chocolate-covered cherries and some peanuts."

Uncle Genald was not married, and he had fallen in love with his sister's kids. He realized Olga was terribly worried about not having money for anything but groceries. She looked at her brother and started to cry. She'd been right. Something had turned up.

Uncle Genald dunked his sugar lump in the last swallow of coffee. His heavy wool jacket felt good as he buttoned it tight around his neck. "Guess I better buckle my overshoes so I don't get my feet wet," he joked, looking at Doris.

A cold blast filled the small room when he opened the door.

---

[*] A soft, flat bread made from mashed potatoes, flour, and cream, rolled out into large, flat circles and baked lightly on a grill

[†] Made like *lefse* but with a firmer, wheat-flour-based dough, rolled thin, baked on a grill, and crisped in a slow oven

[‡] A Norwegian cookie made with eggs, milk, flour, and seasoning, rolled thin, deep-fried until barely brown, and sprinkled with powdered sugar

"Grandma and I will be back on Christmas Eve. We'll see you then," Genald promised as he went out the door.

Doris was already excited. "Goody! Goody!" she said, hurrying to the window to wave good-bye.

As Genald came to the highway corner, he swerved, suddenly deciding to swing into Parshall to look for a small gift for Doris and the boys. He parked in front of Richardson's department store and looked at all the Christmas things. He took his time. Genald was not known to hurry, even if his house might be burning down. He finally settled on a small toy egg beater and a teakettle for Doris and a ball for the boys. He bought a bag of hard Christmas candy for the family. As he climbed into his Model A coupe,* he smiled and began humming "Jingle Bells."

Another Surprise

The next morning, John woke up early and went to town on business. He didn't tell Olga what his plans were. He was looking for a small Christmas tree to bring home as a surprise. With just two days remaining before Christmas Eve, he figured that if any trees were left, they would be marked down.

He pulled up to the empty lot on the edge of town where his friend Edwin was selling trees. Only a few were left. He looked them over, but most of them were still a dollar or more. He could not spend a dollar. Suddenly, he spied a small tree beneath several bigger ones. He pulled it loose, turned it around, and looked at it. "This would be just right on top of the sewing machine in front of the window," he said to Edwin. "How much is this tree?" he asked Edwin.

Edwin looked at the scrawny tree and knew he would've thrown it into the truck with the other unsold trees if John

---

* A two-passenger car with a rear outside hatch that opened and provided seating for two more people

hadn't come. "Well, John," he said, "how about if you just take it? It will be one less tree for me to haul out of here."

John was stunned. "What?" he asked, making sure he'd heard right.

"Just take it, John. You can have it. Your kids will enjoy it."

"Are you sure, Ed? I can pay a little something for it."

"It's yours, John," Edwin said again. "Put it in your car. And have a Merry Christmas, John! You and your family."

"Ya, then. Many thanks, Edwin." John was nearly speechless. "I sure do appreciate it." As John put the tree in the backseat of the car, he turned and yelled to Edwin, "And Merry Christmas to you, too, Edwin, and your family."

John hurried home, anxious to see the looks on the kids' faces. As he turned the corner to go into the yard, he turned the lights and the motor off and coasted to the house. He took the tree out of the car, didn't slam the door, and sneaked into the house.

"Surprise!" he shouted, holding the tree out for all to see.

Doris was the first one to see her daddy open the door.

"A Christmas tree, Daddy? A real Christmas tree?" She danced with delight.

"Goody! Goody!" Jerold and Orin tried not to be too enthusiastic, but they couldn't hide their excitement.

Olga smiled, a bit puzzled, as she wiped her hands on her apron. "Did you decide we could afford to buy a Christmas tree, John?"

John told her what had happened. Olga turned to wipe a tear from her eye, thankful not only for the dollar Genald had given her earlier but for the fact that John had brought home a real Christmas tree. Their Christmas was going to be special after all! She was overcome with joy.

Doris gave her daddy a great big hug. She remembered that last year they had decorated a big Russian thistle for their tree. She could hardly wait for Mama to bring out the small box of decorations hidden high on the shelf in the closet. "Mama, can I help decorate the tree?" Doris begged.

"Of course you can," Olga said. "In fact, you and the boys can do all the decorating."

They ate an early supper so the boys could finish their chores and decorate the tree before bedtime. John fixed a stand for the tree, while Doris helped with the dishes. Jerold and Orin rushed into the house when their chores were finished, took off their jackets, stuffed their caps and mittens in the sleeves, and hung them on the nails by the door.

"Okay, Mama, we're done. What can I do?" Jerold asked.

Doris was already sorting the decorations. "I dubs on putting on all the icicles," she declared.

"Well, then, I'm going to hang the balls. Since you're the oldest, Jerold, you can put the candles on," Orin decided.

"Okay," Jerold agreed without argument.

The boys were just as excited as Doris about having a real Christmas tree standing in the window, but, because they were boys, they didn't jump up and down like their little sister.

"Don't forget, kids," Olga called from the kitchen, where she was popping corn to string, "you can each make a string of popcorn for the tree before bedtime."

By the time they went to bed, they had the tree all decorated. *It looks so pretty,* Doris thought as she looked at it sitting on the sewing machine from the foot of her parents' bed where she slept. Oh, how she loved it. She fell asleep happier than any little girl in the whole world.

Christmas Eve at Last!

"Don't you just love Christmas, Orin?" Doris asked her brother.

"It's okay, I guess," Orin said.

Orin and Jerold kept their excitement to themselves. Even if it was Christmas, they still had chores to do every night. It didn't seem fair that Doris didn't have to do nearly as much work. It seemed to Orin that all she did was play with the presents and rearrange the tinsel on the tree. Neither of the brothers was at all sure that Santa would come to their house, anyway.

On Christmas Eve, Doris woke up earlier than usual. A heavy frost covered the windows. She wanted to get right up, but Olga told her she had to stay in bed where it was warm until the fir in the potbelly stove got started. Doris sighed, turned over, and looked out the frost-covered window. She found all kinds of pretty designs in the frost—a dog, leaves, snowflakes, trees, and many kinds of flowers. *Jack Frost was sure busy,* she thought. *Is there really a Jack Frost?*

After Jerold had put all the candles on the tree where he wanted them, Olga and John reminded the kids to never, ever light the candles. "Only Mama and Daddy will light the candles. Do you three understand?" John said in a loud, gruff voice. The kids nodded and promised.

John lit the candles every night after supper. When Doris woke up each morning, she could hardly wait until it was time to light the candles and sing Christmas carols together before bedtime.

Olga finally told her she could get up and get dressed.

"How long will it be before Grandma and Uncle Genald come?" she asked almost every hour.

"They'll be here for supper," Olga kept telling her.

Doris then went to the tree and sorted and shook the presents again.

When the sun began to set, Doris knew it was time for the boys to do the chores. She kept telling them to hurry and get started, but they ignored her. When they had finished milking, separating the milk, and feeding the calves, they came in and took their jackets and caps off. Then Orin remembered. "Oh, it's Christmas! I have to go back to the barn and give each of the cows a sugar lump," he said. It was a Norwegian tradition.

"Oh, no," Doris said impatiently, hating the thought of another delay. "Do you have to?"

"Sure," Orin said. "It's Christmas!" And out the door he ran, with five sugar lumps in his hand.

To help pass the time, Doris counted the presents under the tree again. She then went to the window in the little bedroom and scraped a small circle of frost off the window so she could watch for Uncle Genald's headlights. She counted all the lights that went by on the main road. Finally, one light seemed to slow down. And it turned. It turned onto their road.

"They're coming, Mama! Their car just turned the corner!"

Olga was also excited. Doris asked if there was anything she could do to help speed things up. "You can put these glasses on the table," Olga told her.

The boys and John were in the house when Genald, Grandma, and Grandpa came in, wishing everyone a Merry Christmas. Finally, Christmas Eve had arrived!

Everyone gathered at the table. After the children said the Norwegian table prayer, Olga began passing around the traditional Christmas Eve food: *lutefisk,** boiled potatoes, creamed carrots and peas, pickles, fresh *lefse*, and flatbread. Rice pudding with lots of whipped cream was served for dessert.

"*Mange tusen takk* for *maten*, Mama," they each said in turn. Olga once again wiped a tear from her eye.

Doris and Grandma helped Olga wash and dry the dishes. As soon as they finished, the grownups pulled chairs close to the tree and watched John light the candles. Jerold and Orin

---

* Lutefisk: Dried cod treated with lye. A Norwegian culinary specialty.

sat on the floor, while Doris sat on her own little chair right next to the presents.

Olga began singing "Silent Night" in Norwegian. Soon everyone joined in.

"Tell us a story about Christmas when you were a little girl in Norway, Grandma," Doris begged.

Grandma Kvam thought for a moment, closed her eyes, and began telling about the little elves who would leave treats by their beds on Christmas Eve and about going to church Christmas morning with a team and sleigh, bundled in deerskin throws.

Uncle Genald and John told funny stories and jokes. Before the presents were opened, Olga read the story of Jesus's birth from the Bible. Grandpa Kvam smiled as the kids sang "Away in a Manger" with all the actions they had learned in Sunday school.

The kids were delighted to find several presents under the tree, including those Uncle Genald and Grandma Kvam had brought and a small package for Genald and Grandma from Olga. Olga and Orin passed out the presents. Doris and Jerold held theirs, waiting anxiously for Mama to tell them when it was their turn to open them.

Doris had shaken and squeezed her package many times, but she hadn't been able to figure out what it could be. Her face lit up like the Christmas tree when she found a pair of long white stockings in a box from Grandma and Grandpa. She had never had long white stockings before, only ugly brown ones that got saggy the second day she wore them.

"Oh, Mama, look! White stockings! Can I wear them to Sunday school? Please?" Many of her friends wore white stockings every Sunday, and Doris could hardly hide her jealousy and envy.

Uncle Genald had wrapped his presents for the kids in brown paper and sneaked them under the tree. It was a surprise even to Olga. When Doris opened her present, she was beside herself. She'd never, *ever* dreamed she would have a toy egg beater and teakettle for her dollhouse. She jumped on Uncle Genald's lap and hugged him.

Jerold and Orin each got a pair of mittens, one brown pair and one blue, which Grandma had knit. Orin quickly put his in his dresser drawer to keep for "good," and Jerold put his under his pillow on the bed he shared with his brother. Both boys thanked Uncle Genald for the ball.

After having coffee and two kinds of Christmas cookies, Grandma and Grandpa Kvam and Uncle Genald left for home. They said good-bye to Olga's family and thanked her for the wonderful Christmas Eve. Jerold, Orin, and Doris started getting ready for bed.

"Will Santa come, Mama?" Doris asked. "Do you really think he knows where we live?"

"Oh, yes, he knows, Doris. He knows if you have been bad or good. He'll come, I'm sure of it. You've been good, haven't you?" Olga asked with a smile.

The three little farm kids were tucked into bed. They said their prayers, the one John had taught them in Norwegian and one they had learned in Sunday school. Soon they were sound asleep, sugar plums dancing in their heads.

Olga knew Santa would not forget their one-room house in the country. She was excited for Santa's visit, too.

Santa Visits the Farm

Olga got out of bed Christmas morning, put a blanket around her shoulders, lit the kerosene lamp in the kitchen, put more kindling and small chunks of coal in the stove, and filled the coffeepot with water. The aroma of coffee brewing was even more special on Christmas morning, it seemed to Olga. She took time to sit in her rocker by the warm heater John had gotten up earlier to stoke. *The cooking can wait,* she told herself.

Orin, Jerold, and Doris woke up earlier than usual and hurried to look under the tree. Olga watched them find the toys Santa had left.

"Look, Mama! Look what Santa brought me!" Doris shrieked as she picked up a little toy broom.

The bag of marbles Santa had left in Jerold's stocking brought a big smile. Marbles were his very favorite game, because he always beat anyone who dared play with him.

Orin actually jumped with joy when he discovered a Chinese checkers game on the floor under his stocking.

"Hey, Jerold," he said, "I know you can beat me in marbles, but I bet you can't beat me in Chinese checkers."

"We'll see!" Jerold laughed.

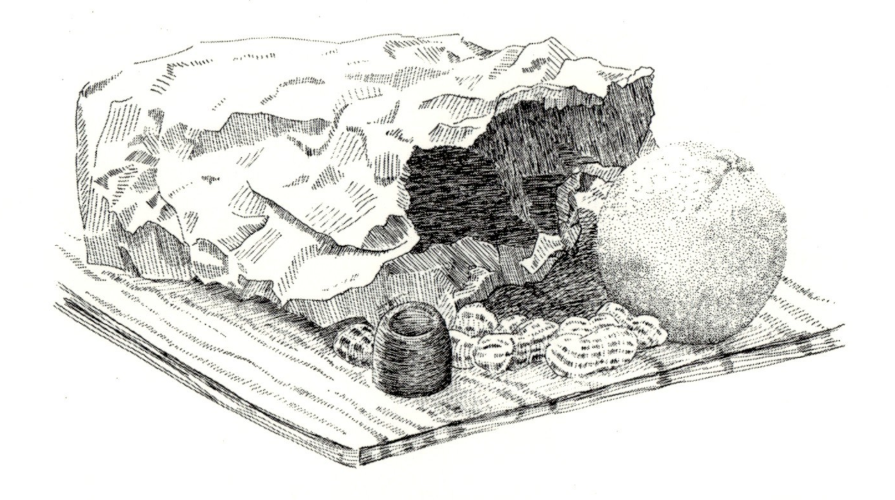

Each of them also found a small brown-paper bag with one chocolate, a few nuts, and an orange inside—all special treats. Jerold saved his chocolate all day by taking only one small bite at a time. He took his last bite before he went to bed that night. But Orin and Doris? They were not quite as disciplined. Their chocolates were in their stomachs before breakfast.

It was a very special Christmas, not only for Jerold, Orin, and Doris, but for Olga and John as well. Many good things had happened, and they silently thanked Jesus for watching over them.

An Unforeseen Disaster

One day after Christmas, Doris was playing with her doll, teakettle, egg beater, and toy broom under the tree. She crinkled pieces of Christmas wrapping paper, put them under the tree, and thought the tree looked even prettier. Then she did what she'd promised she would never do: she lit two candles on the Christmas tree. One of the candles fell off the tree as she was playing with the paper. In a split second, the beautiful crinkled paper was on fire.

Jerold immediately saw what was happening and yelled, "Fire! Fire! Doris started the Christmas tree on fire!"

Mama came running from the shanty and yelled, "Grab a pillow, Jerold! Try to smother the flames! Hurry!"

Orin and Doris ran out of the house and started jumping and yelling. "Daddy! Daddy! The house is on fire! Hurry, Daddy! Run!"

John dropped his pitchfork and ran to the house. John, Olga, and Jerold got the fire out before it lit the house on fire. The Christmas tree, however, was ruined, and most of the decorations were broken and lying on the floor in pieces.

Doris felt like vomiting. She knew she would get a spanking, but she didn't care. All that mattered now was that she hadn't burned the house down.

"I didn't mean to do it—the candle dropped and . . . I . . ." Doris began sobbing uncontrollably, tears streaming down her face.

The fright in Doris's face told her parents she didn't need a spanking.

John took her by the shoulders, shook her gently but firmly, and said, "Don't ever, ever, *ever* do that again! And when Mama and Daddy tell you not to do something, you better not do it!"

"I won't, Daddy! I promise I won't."

Jerold and Orin were watching. Even though they knew Doris had done something very bad, they did not want her to get a spanking. Spankings hurt—badly! They felt sorry for their little sister, and Jerold was almost crying. He had been spanked by Daddy and knew how much it hurt.

Olga took Doris by the hand and put her on her lap. She held her tightly and rocked her until she stopped shaking. "It's okay," Olga kept whispering in her ear. "The house didn't burn down. Shhh. We're safe. It's okay now."

Doris wanted to go to her cot and put her head under the pillow, forever. She didn't want to talk to anybody, especially Jerold, Orin, and Daddy. It was getting dark, and Doris was glad. She could soon go to bed where no one would see her. Mama assured her that she would feel better tomorrow.

At eight o'clock, Olga tucked Doris into bed. Doris started sobbing all over again.

"Mama," she stammered, "I've ruined Christmas! The Christmas tree is burned up, and all the decorations are broken."

"It's all right, Doris. It's over now, and nothing really bad has happened," Olga said.

"Don't worry about the decorations. We can make new ones next year, and you can save some of your money this summer to buy new tinsel." She patted her head until she became quiet and still. "You have learned a very important lesson. You've learned to obey Mama and Daddy, because they always know what's best for you."

Olga was right. Doris had learned some very important lessons. After that Christmas when she was six years old, Doris was always afraid of fire—even when she grew up and became a mama herself.